Beyond Wool

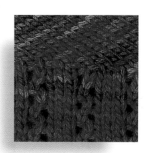

Beyond Wool

25 Knitted Projects using Natural Fibers

CANDACE EISNER STRICK

Martingale®
& COMPANY

Beyond Wool: 25 Knitted Projects
using Natural Fibers
© 2004 by Candace Eisner Strick

Martingale & Company®
20205 144th Avenue NE
Woodinville, WA 98072-8478 USA
www.martingale-pub.com

Printed in China
12 11 10 09 08   8 7 6 5 4 3 2

Strick, Candace Eisner.
    Beyond wool / Candace Eisner Strick.
       p. cm.
    ISBN 978-1-56477-501-6
  1. Knitting—Patterns. I. Title.
    TT820.S88 2004
    746.43'20432—dc22
                                    2003016708

CREDITS

President	*Nancy J. Martin*
CEO	*Daniel J. Martin*
Publisher	*Jane Hamada*
Editorial Director	*Mary V. Green*
Managing Editor	*Tina Cook*
Technical Editor	*Ursula Reikes*
Copy Editor	*Liz McGehee*
Design Director	*Stan Green*
Illustrator	*Robin Strobel*
Cover and Text Designer	*Trina Stahl*
Fashion Photographer	*J. P. Hamel*
Photo Assistant	*Troy Schnyder*
Fashion Stylist	*Susan Huxley*
Hair and Makeup	*Colleen Kobrick*
Studio Photographer	*Brent Kane*

MISSION STATEMENT

Dedicated to providing quality
products and service to inspire creativity.

DEDICATION

To my three sons—Nathaniel, Liam, and Noah—
you are my immortality. L'chayim!

To my husband and the father of my sons—Kenneth L. Strick—
you are the love of my life.

Contents

Introduction

A RECENT KNITTING engagement took me to America's heartland—Kansas. The night before the workshop, the guild had arranged for a little get-together in the hotel lobby. A group of us were happily knitting and chatting when a rather rude man from the bar, which was adjacent to the lobby, started to make fun of us. I'm quite sure he meant no harm and that this was his rather clumsy attempt at flirtation, but his remarks fell short with most of us. I refrained from any comment until he said something about cashmere coming from a sheep. I had just finished writing the chapter on cashmere for this book, and I could no longer keep quiet. I bet him one million dollars that cashmere comes from a goat and not a sheep. Of course, he began to argue with me, and of course I knew he would never pay his debt. In fact, to this day he probably still thinks he's correct. But it got me to thinking that many people—not just rude, one-drink-too-many men—have absolutely no idea where most fibers come from. Fortunately, most knitters have a wider range of knowledge about fibers than my boorish Kansas flirt, since they have the opportunity to knit with the huge variety of fibers that are now available. I found, though, that the pleasure of working with these fibers is further enhanced by really knowing the story of where they come from and how they are produced. The animals themselves are a source of delight to me, and how much more wonderful that yarn feels when I have actually met the animal who gave it to me!

The thought of designing with luxury fibers was overwhelmingly appealing. I must admit, the experience was everything I thought it would be. I marvel at the gigantic steps the fiber industry has taken since the 1960s, when I began knitting seriously. A knitter then had the choice of three weights of yarn. I don't recall any blends, and I don't recall any more than just a handful of specific brands and a very limited color palette. I also had a whole new experience open up to me now that I know the delights of plant fibers and the opportunities they offer for warm-weather knitting. I have tried to match a particular design with what would best show off the unique properties of each of the yarns.

It is my fondest wish that more and more people will recognize the wonderful pleasures gained not only from knitting, but also by the unique and close network that knitters establish. We are a diverse group of people brought together by our common interest, and the riches gained from this alone are worth the price of cashmere! When one is being creative, there is no time for anything negative. Our minds and hands are occupied, we are content and satisfied, and for a few brief stolen minutes, the outside pressures and strife in the world are forgotten. Never, NEVER, feel guilty for buying yarn that you are attracted to, and never underestimate the powers of your fiber and knitting, for they are powerful healers.

Mohair

Angora Goats (Photo by Kenneth Strick)

THE WORD *mohair* simply means the finest or best fiber. It is a remarkably long fiber that is soft yet strong, flame-retardant, accepts dye incredibly well, and has a luster that is unsurpassed by any other animal fiber. Besides its use in sweaters, mohair crops up in such unsuspecting places as carpeting, men's suiting, doll hair, Santa's beards, blankets, outerwear, rugs, and upholstery. This remarkable fiber is produced by a small and hardy little fellow called an Angora goat.

Not to be confused with the Angora rabbit, which produces a fiber called angora, Angora goats produce mohair. Originally from the Ankara region of Turkey, the first goats in America were a gift from the Sultan of Turkey in 1849. Raised for their luxury hair, a single adult goat can produce between 10 and 25 pounds of fiber per year. Shearing is usually done twice a year. If the animals are not sheared, the hair keeps growing at an approximate rate of one inch per month, hanging down the sides of the animal in curly, corkscrew locks.

Kid mohair, prized for its softness, is the first clipping of a one-year-old goat. The average yield is usually only about 4 pounds. The micron range of each fiber is about 18–20. With each successive clipping, the fiber becomes coarser, with a higher micron number. Angora goat breeders today are challenged with trying to breed a goat whose hair will stay soft as it gets older.

Angora goats are at home in Turkey, on the range in Texas, or in the lush rolling hills of New England. The largest producer of mohair is South Africa. The United States ranks second, with Texas producing 90% of the country's supply. Turkey ranks third. Most of the mohair raised in this country is shipped overseas, manufactured into finished products, and then shipped back for resale. The goats are small, hardy, and require shelter only in very wet weather. In the northeastern United States, 20 to 30 acres of pasture can sustain about 100 goats. In Texas, it takes about 200 to 300 acres for the same number of animals. The land they graze on is land that cannot support any other type of animal. Life in Texas is hard for the goats, and it's not unusual to see one actually climbing a tree in order to get at the leaves. In contrast, their New England cousins have checked into a four-star hotel! While the majority of Angora goats are raised for their fiber, some are used for meat.

Before the actual spinning process, mohair must first go through a series of preparations. The heavy lanolin-type substance on Angora goats requires the hair to be scoured in very hot water: 160 to 180 degrees Fahrenheit. For the commercial machinery to spin the fiber, it must be completely free of this waxy grease. It is interesting to note that this heavy grease has, throughout history, played an important part in the price of the clip. The greasier the coat, the more it weighs. Because the clip is sold by the pound, it was advantageous to the farmer to breed a goat with large amounts of grease in its fiber.

After the scouring, the fibers are then combed or carded, depending on the spinning method that will be used. For a worsted method, the hair is pulled through combs and draw frames. The more times this is done, the more parallel the fibers become. For a true worsted method, the noil (very short pieces of the hair) is removed. Yarn spun by this method is very smooth and less fluffy than yarn spun in the woolen method, in which the fibers are not kept parallel.

Sara Healy and Dan Melamed raise 65 Angora goats a year on their farm in Germantown, New York. Wanting to take advantage of the very long fiber and to preserve its incredible luster, they wanted their 100% mohair yarn to be spun in the worsted method. Most mills, however, have a problem spinning the long fibers because they are very slippery. Dan and Sara finally found a mill that could do what they call "semi-worsted," a process that is like true worsted but lacks the one extra step of removing the noil. They have their fiber spun into both two-ply and three-ply. Pick up one of these skeins and be prepared to be amazed! The light bounces off this stuff and gives it a luster that is akin to silk. A denser fiber than wool, mohair yields fewer yards per pound than wool when spun into yarn. An 8-ounce skein of 100% mohair is about the same size as a 4-ounce skein of worsted wool. Besides the beautiful, creamy white natural color, Sara hand dyes some of the skeins into rich and seductive colors, using only natural dyes. Angora goats do come in a variety of natural colors, ranging from the common white to the less common shades of gray and even chestnut.

Wanting to perfect their spin even more, Sara and Dan are in the process of purchasing their own spinning equipment. Before leaving Dan and Sara and their flock of goats, I asked what special treats the animals like. Sara told me they love potato chips, and in fact, when it comes time to give them their worming medicine, they sandwich the worm paste between two potato chips!

KNITTING AND DESIGNING WITH MOHAIR

KNITTING with 100% mohair is an experience. Because the scales on the fiber are bigger, flatter, and farther apart than the scales on wool, it does not stick to itself as well and therefore does not felt as well. The scale arrangement does, however, give it incredible luster, as the light is reflected off the surface area of the scales. If felting is the desired outcome, be sure to choose a blend that has wool in it. The inelasticity of mohair results from the crimp of the locks being farther apart than that of wool. Stitches must be worked a little more firmly, and any pattern that works up smoothly in another yarn may not look quite as smooth in mohair, as the inelasticity makes it harder to get a consistent tension.

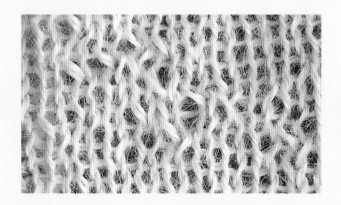

Notice the uneven stitches in this sample.

By blending varying amounts of mohair with wool and/or other fibers, some of these properties are overcome. In choosing a stitch pattern for the Edelweiss Jacket (page 20), I was aiming for something that would give the fabric some elasticity. The obvious choice was ribbing, but with 100% mohair, it is virtually impossible to get a smooth, even stockinette fabric. Since ribbing is basically 50% stockinette stitch, my vertical columns of knit were uneven and not at all tidy looking.

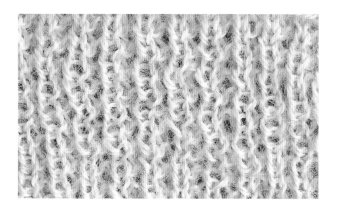

Ribbing done in mohair results in an uneven pattern.

The solution was to break up those vertical lines by incorporating a line of something that was not smooth.

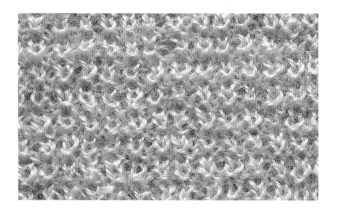

A ridge of garter stitch breaks up the ribbing to produce a smoother pattern.

Bouclé is produced by spinning mohair onto a core yarn of usually wool and nylon. The mohair is fed onto the core at a faster speed, produc-

ing the characteristic loops. Almost every knitter knows that it is foolhardy to try to work any textured pattern in bouclé, as it almost never shows up.

Pattern stitches are barely visible in bouclé.

With the beautifully hand-dyed bouclé from Oak Grove Yarns, I decided that something ultra-simple would be the best bet for the Bouclé Swing Coat (page 14). Reverse stockinette stitch gives a subtle texture and lets the beauty of the colors make the statement.

Reverse stockinette stitch is used in the body of the coat.

I still wanted something more interesting, though, especially around the bottom of the coat. Using the 100% silk that matches the bouclé, I was able to create a welted effect for the borders.

Mohair's fluffiness is actually the by-product of its slickness. After the fiber is spun, some of it invariably slips out of the twist, creating a haze of fluff. If more fluff is desired, it is then brushed by passing it between two drums of fine needles. It is best worked at a very loose tension, or in a lace pattern, as the fluffiness makes a lovely haze over the holes of the knitting.

The beautiful Douceur et Soie from K1C2, a blend of 70% baby mohair and 30% silk, makes an ethereal shawl when worked in garter stitch on big needles. The fine diameter of the yarn makes a shawl that can pass through a wedding band, and the silk gives it a subtle sheen. I could have selected a simple lace pattern for Clouds of Purple Shawl (page 18), but the luxury of the yarn made me want to pause and just savor the pleasure of knitting with it.

Clouds of Purple Shawl is fine enough to fit through a wedding band.

Bouclé Swing Coat

BEAUTIFUL HAND-DYED mohair from Oak Grove Yarns was the inspiration for this kicky and fun swing coat. Done in simple reverse stockinette stitch on size 7 needles, it knits up fast and easy. It gets its swing from the unique shaping that is done by decreasing along triangular shapes that extend from the hem to the waist. The lower welting on the hems of the coat and sleeves make a dramatic design statement. Linda MacMillan, of Oak Grove Yarns, explains that the yarn is spun in the same manner as brushed mohair, but is not brushed. This makes for smallish loops along the core and a fine, silky feel. The dyed-to-match 100% silk used in the welting and button band silk is the perfect companion to this luxurious yarn.

Materials

- 24 (28, 32, 34) ounces, 1500 (1750, 2000, 2125) yards Kid Mohair Bouclé from Oak Grove Yarns (80% kid mohair, 12% wool, 8% nylon), color Falling Leaves, or other worsted-weight yarn
- 340 (390, 440, 490) yards 100% Silk from Oak Grove Yarns, color Falling Leaves, or other light, worsted-weight yarn
- Size 7 (4.5 mm) needles or size needed to obtain gauge
- Size 5 (3.75 mm) needles
- Size E/4 (3.5 mm) crochet hook
- 5 buttons, ¾" diameter
- 1 set of shoulder pads
- Stitch markers

Gauge

16 sts and 25 rows = 4" in reverse stockinette stitch on size 7 needles

Finished Measurements

Bust: 42½ (44, 46, 47½)"
Center Back Length: 32¼ (32½, 33, 33½)"

Pattern Stitches

Reverse Stockinette Stitch
Row 1 (WS): Knit.
Row 2 (RS): Purl.

Stockinette Stitch
Row 1 (RS): Knit.
Row 2 (WS): Purl.

Welting Pattern
Rows 1–19: Work rev St st with bouclé.
Rows 20–23: Work St st with silk.
Row 24: Knit with bouclé.
Rows 25–29: Work rev St st with bouclé.
Rows 30–33: Work St st with silk.

Row 34: Knit with bouclé.
Rows 35–39: Work rev St st with bouclé.
Rows 40–43: Work St st with silk.
Row 44: Knit with bouclé.
Rows 45–49: Work rev St st with bouclé.
Rows 50–53: Work St st with silk.
Row 54: Knit with bouclé.
Rows 55–59: Work rev St st with bouclé.
Rows 60–63: Work St st with silk.
Row 64: Knit with bouclé.
Rows 65–144: Work rev St st with bouclé.

Back

- With size 7 needle and bouclé, CO 25 (27, 30, 32) sts, pm, CO 16 sts, pm, CO 36 sts, pm, CO 16 sts, pm, CO 25 (27, 30, 32) sts—118 (122, 128, 132) sts.
- Work 143 rows in welting patt, working dec on rows 18, 36, 56, 72, 90, 108, and 126 as foll: purl to marker, *sl marker, P2tog, purl to 2 sts before marker, P2tog, sl marker*, purl to next marker, rep from * to *, purl to end of row (4-st dec).
- Work row 144 as foll: purl to marker, **remove marker, P2tog, remove marker**, purl to next marker, rep from ** to **, purl to end of row—88 (92, 98, 102) sts. The rem of the piece is worked in rev St st.
- Work even until piece measures 18½" from last row of silk St st.
- **Shape armholes:** BO 3 sts at beg of next 2 (2, 4, 4) rows, 2 sts at beg of next 4 (6, 4, 6) rows, dec 1 st at each side EOR 2 (1, 2, 1) times—70 (72, 74, 76) sts.
- Work even until armhole measures 9¼ (9½, 10, 10½)", ending with a completed WS row.
- **Shape shoulders and neck (RS):** Work 20 (21, 22, 23) sts, BO middle 30 sts, work rem 20 (21, 22, 23) sts. Work each side separately.
- **Left side (WS):** At beg of next 3 WS rows, BO as foll: 6 (7, 7, 7) sts, 7 (7, 7, 8) sts, and 7 (7, 8, 8) sts.

- **Right side (WS):** Attach yarn at neck edge and work 1 row. Work as for left side, BO for shoulders on RS rows.

RIGHT FRONT

- With size 7 needle and bouclé, CO 25 (27, 30, 32) sts, pm, CO 16 sts, pm, CO 22 sts— 63 (65, 68, 70) sts.
- Work as for back, working one set of decs from * to * as for back, until armhole shaping, ending with a completed RS row—48 (50, 53, 55) sts.
- **Shape armholes:** (WS) BO 3 sts at beg of next 1 (1, 2, 2) WS rows, 2 sts at beg of next 2 (3, 2, 3) WS rows, dec 1 st at beg of each WS row 2 (1, 2, 1) times—39 (40, 41, 42) sts.
- Work even until armhole measures 7½ (7¾, 8, 8¼)", ending with a completed WS row.
- **Shape neck:** BO 5 sts at beg of next RS row, BO at same edge every RS row as foll: 4 sts, 3 sts, and (2 sts) 3 times, then BO 1 st—20 (21, 22, 23) sts.
- Work even until armhole measures same as back to beg of shoulder shaping. BO shoulders as for back.

LEFT FRONT

- With size 7 needle and bouclé, CO 22 sts, pm, CO 16 sts, pm, CO 25 (27, 30, 32) sts— 63 (65, 68, 70) sts.
- Work as for right front; reversing shaping.

SLEEVES

- With size 7 needle and bouclé, CO 54 (58, 60, 64) sts. Patt for sleeve is rows 1–44 of welting pattern, then rev St st for rem of sleeve.

- Inc 1 st at each side every 8 rows 9 times, then every 6 rows 2 times—76 (80, 82, 86) sts.
- Work even until piece measures 11" from last St st silk stripe, ending with a completed WS row.
- **Shape cap:** BO 3 sts at beg of next 2 rows, BO 2 sts at beg of next 4 (8, 10, 14) rows, dec 1 st at each side EOR 19 (17, 16, 14) times, BO 2 sts at beg of next 2 rows, BO 3 sts at beg of next 2 rows. BO rem 14 sts.

FINISHING

- Sew shoulder seams firmly. Sew side seams. Sew side seams of sleeves, then sew sleeves into armholes. With silk, crochet hook, and WS facing, sc through both thicknesses all around armhole and shoulder seams to stabilize them.
- **Right front band:** With silk and size 5 needle, CO 6 sts.
  Row 1 (WS): K6.
  Row 2: Wyib sl 1 pw, P5.
  Rep the last 2 rows 9 times, work row 1. Work the foll 2 rows 120 times (or until band, stretched slightly, is the correct length):
  Row 1 (RS): Wyif sl 1 pw, K5.
  Row 2: K6.
  BO. Sew the nonslipped-st edge of band to right front of sweater with the rev St st of the band at the bottom of the garment, stretching the band slightly to fit.
- **Left front band:** With silk and size 5 needle, CO 6 sts.
  Row 1 (WS): Wyib sl 1 pw, K5.
  Row 2: P6.
  Rep the last 2 rows 9 times, work row 1.

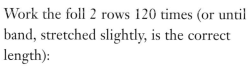

Work the foll 2 rows 120 times (or until band, stretched slightly, is the correct length):

Row 1 (RS): K6.

Row 2: Wyif sl 1 pw, K5.

BO. Sew to left side.

Crochet edging (with button loops) and stabilizing: With silk, crochet hook, and starting at lower edge of right front band, sc in each sl st on band up to neck edge, ch 1, turn, sc into each sc to lower edge of band, ch 1, turn, sc in each of next 60 sc, work button loops as foll: (ch 5, sc in each of next 15 sc) 4 times, ch 5, sc in each of next 2 sc. Ch 1, sc in each st at top of right band, then work 23 sc around neck to shoulder seam, work 29 sc around back neck to other shoulder seam, work 23 sc around neck to top of left band, 1 sc in each st at top of left band.

Ch 1, sc in each sl st of left band to lower edge, ch 1, turn, sc in each sc to neck edge, ch 1, turn, sc in each sc back to lower edge. Fasten off. Lightly tack lower edges of bands to match the rev St st curl of hem.

Neck: With size 5 needle, silk, and WS facing, PU 1 st in each sc around neck edge. With bouclé and RS facing, knit 1 row. Work 19 rows of St st. BO very loosely. The collar will roll over on itself, revealing the rev St st side.

Wash and lay flat to dry, pinning center front bands so that they are even. Do not pull welting so that it flattens out; let it dry slightly scrunched up.

Sew buttons to left band to correspond with button loops.

Sew in shoulder pads.

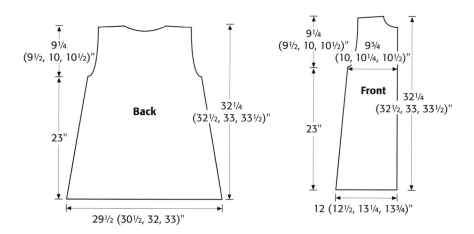

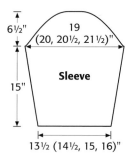

Clouds of Purple Shawl

NOTHING COULD BE more ethereal than this featherlight shawl done in a stunning plum shade with the incredible luxury of this mohair and silk yarn. The six increases every two rows elongate the tails for a graceful tie in the front and just a hint of shoulder draping. Try pulling it through a wedding ring. It passes the test!

MATERIALS

- 4 skeins Douceur et Soie from K1C2 (70% baby mohair, 30% silk; 25 grams, 225 yards per skein), color Plum, or other fingering-weight yarn
- Size 7 (4.5 mm) circular needle (29") or size needed to obtain gauge
- Size E/4 (3.50 mm) crochet hook
- Stitch markers

GAUGE

18 sts and 36 rows = 4" in garter stitch on size 7 needles

FINISHED MEASUREMENTS

CENTER BACK LENGTH: 23" (blocked)

TOTAL WIDTH (measured across back neck to wing sides): 44"

PATTERN STITCH

Garter Stitch

Knit every row.

SHAWL

NOTE: For M1, make a firm backward loop on the needle (see page 128).

- CO 1 st, pm, CO 1 st, pm, CO 1 st—3 sts. Knit 1 row.
- **Row 1:** YO, K1, M1, sl marker, knit center st, sl marker, M1, K1—6 sts.
- **Row 2:** YO, knit to end of row—7 sts.
- **Row 3:** YO, K1, M1, knit to marker, M1, sl marker, knit center st, sl marker, M1, knit to last st, M1, K1—12 sts.
- **Row 4:** YO, knit to end of row—13 sts.
- Rep rows 3 and 4 until you have 367 sts—183 + 1 + 183 sts. Five incs have been made on every odd-numbered row and 1 inc on every even-numbered row.
- **BO as foll:** sl first st to crochet hook, *ch 5, sl next st to crochet hook, YO and pull through both sts on hook*, rep from * to * until all sts are used up. Break yarn and pull through last st.

FINISHING

This shawl is shaped so it will stay on your shoulders. Do not block straight across the top, but block the top edge in a gentle U shape.

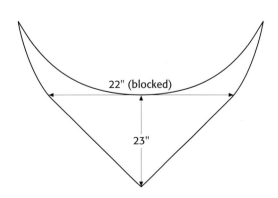

22" (blocked)

23"

Edelweiss Jacket

THE SIMPLE SHAPE of this jacket reminds me of traditional Bavarian jackets made from boiled wool. When worked in 100% mohair, this easy pattern stitch looks deceptively like double knit. Show it to your friends and challenge them to figure out the pattern!

MATERIALS

- 6 (6, 7) skeins Mohair from Buckwheat Bridge (100% mohair; 4 ounces, 220 yards per skein), Creamy Natural White, or other sport-weight yarn
- Size 2 (2.75 mm) circular needle (29" or longer)
- One set of 7"-long double-pointed needles, size 2 (2.75 mm)
- Size 3 (3.25 mm) circular needle (29") or size needed to obtain gauge
- 5 stitch markers (4 the same color, 1 different)
- 1 clasp (or more if desired)

GAUGE

22 sts and 40 rows = 4" in pattern stitch on size 3 needles

FINISHED MEASUREMENTS

Bust: 40 (44, 48)"
Center Back Length: 21 (22, 24)"

PATTERN STITCH

Note: This pattern stitch is reversible. Be sure to mark the RS of your work.

Row 1 (RS): *K1, P1*, rep from * to * to last st, K1.
Row 2 (WS): *P1, K1*, rep from * to * to last st, P1.
Rows 3 and 4: Knit.
Rep rows 1–4.

BACK

- With size 3 needle, CO 111 (121, 131) sts.
- Work in patt for 12 (13, 14)".

- **Shape armholes:** BO 9 (9, 10) sts at beg of next 2 rows, dec 1 st at each side every RS row 9 (9, 10) times—75 (85, 91) sts. Cont in patt until armhole measures 8 (8, 9)", ending with a completed RS row.
- **Shape back neck and shoulders:** Cont in patt, work 21 (25, 27) sts, join second ball of yarn and BO 33 (35, 37) sts for back neck, work rem 21 (25, 27) sts. Working both sides at once, BO as foll: 6 (7, 8) sts at beg of next 2 rows, 6 (8, 8) sts at beg of next 2 rows, AT SAME TIME dec 1 st at each side of neck every WS row twice. Beg at armhole edge, BO rem 7 (8, 9) sts on each shoulder.

LEFT FRONT

- With size 3 needle, CO 55 (61, 65) sts. Work as for back until piece measures 12 (13, 14)", ending with a completed WS row.
- **Shape armhole:** BO 9 (9, 10) sts at beg of next row, dec 1 st at armhole edge every RS row 9 (9, 10) times 37 (43, 45) sts. Cont in patt until armhole measures 8 (8, 9)", ending with a completed RS row.
- **Shape neck:** BO 11 (13, 13) sts at beg of WS row, dec 1 st at neck every WS row 7 times. Work 4 (4, 8) rows even—19 (23, 25) sts for shoulder. BO shoulder as for back.

RIGHT FRONT

Work as for left front, reversing shaping.

SLEEVES

- With size 3 needle, CO 49 (51, 53) sts. Work in patt, inc 1 st at each side every 8 rows 12 times, then every 10 rows 7 times— 87 (89, 91) sts.
- Work 2 (6, 8) rows even.

- **Shape cap:** BO 9 (9, 10) sts at beg of next 2 rows, dec 1 st at each side every RS row 18 times, then every 3 rows 4 (4, 5) times—25 (27, 25) sts.
- **BO as foll:** 2 (3, 2) sts at beg of next 2 rows, 2 sts at beg of next 2 rows. BO rem 17 sts.

FINISHING

- Sew shoulder and side seams.
- Sew sleeve seams and sew sleeves into armholes.
- **Body border:** With RS facing, size 2 circ needle, and beg at right side seam, PU 109 (119, 129) sts along back bottom, 53 (59, 63) sts along left front bottom, pm, 96 (106, 118) sts along left front, pm, 29 (31, 35) sts along left front neck to shoulder, 33 (35, 37) sts along back neck to other shoulder, 29 (31, 35) sts along right front neck, pm, 96 (106, 118) sts along right front, pm, 53 (59, 63) sts along right front bottom—498 (546, 598) sts. Join rnd by slipping last st over first and putting first st on RH needle. Place a different colored marker here to mark the beg and end of rnd. Turn work and knit 4 rnds (making rev St st on RS), inc 1 st on each side of 4 corner markers on rnds 2 and 4 (16 sts increased). BO very loosely.
- **Sleeve border:** With size 2 dpn, beg at underarm seam, PU 49 (51, 53) sts. Work as for body border, omitting inc.
- Sew 1 clasp just below neck. If desired, add additional clasps spaced evenly down front.

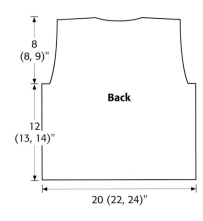

8 (8, 9)"

Back

12 (13, 14)"

20 (22, 24)"

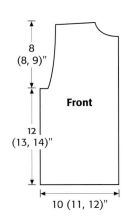

8 (8, 9)"

Front

12 (13, 14)"

10 (11, 12)"

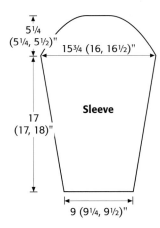

5¼ (5¼, 5½)"

15¾ (16, 16½)"

Sleeve

17 (17, 18)"

9 (9¼, 9½)"

Alpaca and Llama

Alpacas (Photo by Candace Strick)

GRACEFULLY elegant, alpacas are gentle and inquisitive creatures that give us soft, luxurious wool. They display an amazing range of natural colors, and the markings on their faces often seem to give them quizzical expressions.

ALPACA

HIGH in the altiplano of South America, at an elevation of 14,000 feet or more, alpacas graze on the sparse vegetation as they did thousands of years ago. Alpacas were central to the Andean way of life in 4,000 B.C. They were used for sacrificial ceremonies, food, and fiber. The shepherds of the Andean culture selectively bred their animals for maximum fiber quality and color. When the Spanish conquistadors invaded the area in 1532, they demolished not only the human population but almost 90% of the entire world's population of alpacas. Since only a limited number of animals survived, composing a very small gene pool, the arduous task of selective breeding had to begin over.

Alpacas are members of the Camelidae family, all of which possess a double coat. Within the one species of alpaca there are two distinct types, distinguished by their coats of fiber. The Huacaya (wha-ki-ya) has a shorter, denser coat while the Suri has long, luxurious locks. There are 22 official classified colors, but probably more than 100 different hues, ranging from jet black to snow white.

These beautiful animals have long necks and slender legs, padded cloven hooves, and large round eyes with incredibly long eyelashes. They are inquisitive, alert, gentle creatures that can survive in places where the climate is harsh and vegetation is sparse. An estimated 2.5 million alpacas are alive today, with 80% of them owned by the indigenous people of the highlands of southern Peru and Bolivia. The remaining 20% are owned by agricultural cooperatives and private individuals.

Prior to 1989, all the alpacas in the United States were regarded as exotic pets. They could be bought in Peru for $200 to $300 and sold here for $12,000 to $28,000. The demand for them was so great that a lottery for exporting them had to be instituted. The primary market now is for breeding and selling. A quality alpaca can fetch a price of $60,000; stud fees can be anywhere from $2,000 to $3,000. The secondary market is fiber. For many, raising alpaca is more a lifestyle than a moneymaker.

Linda Niemeyer knit a pair of alpaca mittens, felted them, and sold them for $70. This was the beginning of her love affair with these beautiful animals, and she has found happiness in the alpaca lifestyle. She presently has 11 alpacas on her farm just south of Minneapolis, Minnesota. Linda shears her animals once a year and keeps all the fiber. She and her mother hand spin it. The commercially spun skeins of alpaca she sells for her business, Blue Sky Alpacas, is imported from Bolivia. For Linda, alpaca fiber is the best. It takes dye extremely well; it is shiny, silky, and has a wondrous luster. It spans the seasons better than wool, because it breathes so well. In Linda's words, "It is fluid and elegant, drapes beautifully, and catches the light."

To be desirable, the fiber produced by an animal must have a low micron count. One micron is equal to 1/1000 of a millimeter, or 1/25,400 of an inch. To get a better idea of how tiny one micron is, think of it this way: Divide one inch in half, then divide that half in half, then divide that half in half. Now divide that half into 3,175 equal parts. One of those parts is equal to one micron! As a comparison, the average human hair can be between 40 and 80 microns; superfine alpaca is about 26 microns; the average baby alpaca is 22 microns. Once the micron count gets 30 or above, the "prickle" factor on human skin becomes apparent. Vicuña, a relative of the alpaca, has the lowest micron count of any animal: 11. Unfortunately, the government of Peru does not allow export of the fiber.

Micron count can be directly related to several things: heredity, color, and diet. Light-colored animals on the whole tend to have finer hair than darker animals. Animals that feed on a very lean diet tend to have a lower micron count. In fact, in switching diets from lean to abundant, the count can go up as much as 8 or 9 microns in less than a year's time. The trick is to keep your alpaca happy and well while at the same time striving for a low micron count. Kathy Haneke, founder and proprietress of Haneke Wool Fashions, raises alpacas on her farm in Meridian, Idaho. The alpaca she uses in her signature yarn, Heaven Sent, is a blend of 70% baby royal alpaca and 30% wool and has the cloud-soft micron count of 17.

Kathy's alpaca training has been intensive and diverse. Her studies have taken her from one end of Chile to the other. On a recent trip to Peru, she taught alpaca farmers how to use fiber shears. Traditionally, one man would grab the neck of the alpaca and wrestle it down to lay it on its side. While this man straddles the front neck, three women shear it using the sharpened lids of sardine cans. After a lesson with the shears, two men were able to shear one alpaca in less time and with much less damage to the animal.

After the shearing, alpaca fiber goes through much the same process as wool before it is spun: cleaning, carding, and dyeing. Because the fiber is so slippery, it takes specialized spinning equipment, and very few mills in this country own the proper equipment. Kathy's solution was to buy her own mill. Shearing takes place in May at Kathy's farm, and everyone with four legs gets a haircut, including the cat!

Kathy loves to blend her exotic fibers, believing each individual fiber adds its own special characteristics to the resulting yarn. For instance, alpaca is basically inelastic, but if you blend a small amount of merino wool with it, you get the best of both worlds. Mixing alpaca with linen gives the linen the softness it needs, and the linen, in turn, imparts a sheen and crispness to the alpaca. Kathy laughs when she says that that she has tried to blend every fiber known to mankind, including dryer lint! I silently wonder about that sheared cat I saw walk by a few minutes ago.

Llama

Author Hugging Very Friendly Llama, Chicolita

(Photo by Linda Niemeyer)

THE alpaca's cousin, the llama, is slightly bigger and taller, weighing around 300 pounds and standing about 5 to 6 feet tall. The Inca civilization used them as pack animals and for the same resources as alpaca. Introduced in the United States 100 years ago, they are used by sheep farmers as guardians and by hikers as pack animals. If llamas feel that the load is too heavy or they've worked hard enough for the day, they will kneel down and refuse to budge! When they are upset or scared, they may spit. When they are content, they make a humming sound, much like a cat's purring.

DESIGNING AND KNITTING WITH ALPACA AND LLAMA

ALPACA is a soft and lovely fiber that is a joy to work with, producing a lovely haze of fine fluff over the knitted fabric.

With Blue Sky Alpacas's beautiful colors in front of me, I decided on a hat and mitten set. I used the idea of chevrons because the placement of the increases and decreases achieves automatic

shaping for the top of the mitten. Using the same method for a hat, I was delighted by the unusual shape. Two different looks can be achieved by wearing the hat with the chevrons either in the front or on the sides.

The very fine fluffy haze is evident in these mittens.

With the 50% alpaca/50% silk used in the Ice Blue Shell (page 30), I needed a stitch pattern that would impart some elasticity, but I didn't want ribbing. A slip-stitch pattern proved to be the perfect choice, giving the garment incredible lateral stretch but allowing it to spring back to its original size. The vertical lines needed nothing on the bottom for finishing, and the neckline and armholes required only reverse stockinette stitch. Season-spanning and versatile, this shell can go under a jacket during winter, go solo in summer, or be paired with a lacy shawl for cooler evenings.

A simple stitch pattern produces a lovely design in the Ice Blue Shell.

Kathy Haneke's Heaven Sent yarn has 30% wool blended with the royal baby alpaca. This small amount of wool gives the alpaca the elasticity it lacks, yet does not take away from its beautifully soft hand. Knowing that elasticity and stretch were not going to be a problem, I set about designing a sweater with virtually any stitch pattern I wanted. I envisioned a sweater that was somewhat dressy, since the yarn was so elegantly beautiful. For the Heavenly Blue Cardigan (page 33), I chose a small cable-and-lace pattern. I wanted a firm lower edging but did not want the draw-in that occurs with ribbing. I also wanted side slits that would require no finishing. After much experimenting, I came up with a horizontal welted pattern interrupted by vertical lines of stockinette. I was able to achieve the same gauge with both of the differing patterns by using a slip stitch within the vertical lines. The slip stitch also proved to be the perfect finishing at the side vents, because it gently rolled the last vertical columns to the wrong side of the fabric. The sweater was a delight to knit. The pattern was easily memorized and the yarn slipping through my fingers was a pleasure I did not want to end!

The Cascade Pastaza is a blend of 50% llama and 50% wool. The wool content gives the llama the elasticity it lacks, thereby making it perfectly suited for almost any stitch pattern. For Llama Cables (page 37), I chose an allover cabled pattern, which makes a very formfitting but stretchy sweater. To avoid disturbing the vertical lines of the cables, I chose an uncomplicated shape with a funnel neckline.

Unstretched Cables

The border pattern in Heavenly Blue Cardigan includes side vents for a comfortable fit.

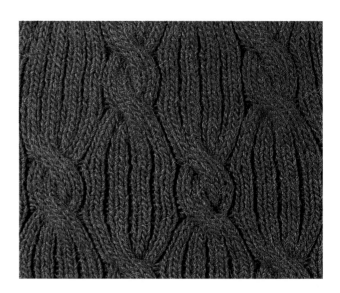

Stretched Cables

Blue Sky Mittens and Hat

ONCE YOU HAVE worked one pair of these mittens according to the directions below, you will feel confident to branch out and make them to custom-fit any size hand. The beginning triangle determines the circumference. After that, you are free to make the thumb opening anywhere you want, and the length to fit any size hand. The cuff can be as fancy or as plain as you wish, long or short.

Wear your hat with either the triangle in the front or to the side. Flop the top part over any which way. Directions are given for one size only: women's size Medium.

MATERIALS

For Mittens or Hat Only

- Sport Weight Alpaca from Blue Sky Alpacas (100% alpaca; 2 ounces, 120 yards per skein), or other sport-weight yarn in each of the following amounts and colors:

1 skein	Red #23
1 skein	Black #100
1 skein	Light Gray #009

For Mittens and Hat

2 skeins	Red #23
1 skein	Black #100
1 skein	Light Gray #009

- One 7"-long set of 5 double-pointed needles, size 3 (3.25 mm) or size needed to obtain gauge
- One 10"-long set of 5 double-pointed needles, size 3 (3.25 mm)
- Stitch markers
- Stitch holder

GAUGE

28 sts and 36 rnds = 4" in stockinette stitch on size 3 needles

FINISHED MEASUREMENTS (WOMEN'S SIZE MEDIUM)

MITTEN LENGTH: 10¼"
MITTEN CIRCUMFERENCE: 7½"
HAT CIRCUMFERENCE: 22"
HAT HEIGHT: 9½"

PATTERN STITCH

Rnds 1–4: With light gray, knit.
Rnds 5–10: With black, knit.
Rnds 11–12: With light gray, knit.
Rnds 13–18: With red, knit.
Rep these 18 rnds for patt.

RIGHT MITTEN

NOTE: M1 by making a firm backward loop onto needle (see page 128).

- **Beg triangle:** With red and 7" dpn, CO 1 st, pm, CO 1 st, pm, CO 1 st—3 sts.
  Row 1: K1, M1, sl marker, knit center st, sl marker, M1, K1; (2 + 1 + 2)—5 sts.
  Row 2: Knit.
  Row 3: K1, M1, K1, M1, sl marker, knit center st, sl marker, M1, K1, M1, K1; (4 + 1 + 4)—9 sts.
  Row 4: Knit.
  Row 5: K1, M1, knit to marker, M1, sl marker, knit center st, sl marker, M1, knit to last st, M1, K1; (6 + 1 + 6)—13 sts.
  Row 6: Knit.
  Rep rows 5 and 6 until there are 14 + 1 + 14 sts (29 sts), ending with a completed row 6. Break yarn.
- Make another triangle exactly like the one above, but do not break yarn at end.

Join triangles: Use red that is still attached to the second triangle as your working yarn. Working the first row will distribute the sts onto 4 needles as foll:

Rnd 1, needle 1: SSK, knit to center st, inc 1 st by making a firm backward loop onto needle, sl marker, knit center st.

Rnd 1, needle 2: M1 (by lifting horizontal running thread between the sts and knit into the back of it), knit to last 2 sts of triangle, K2tog.

Rnd 1, needle 3: Rep as for needle 1 using the other triangle.

Rnd 1, needle 4: Rep as for needle 2 using the other triangle.

Rnd 2: Knit.

Keeping sts in this needle distribution, rep these 2 rnds in patt for 18 rnds.

Right thumb opening: Keeping in color patt, work first 3 sts of needle 1, place next 6 sts onto holder, CO 6 sts. Cont working above 2 rnds in patt for 28 more rnds.

Shape top:

Rnd 1 for all needles: Same as above.

Rnd 2: SSK at beg of needle 1, knit to last 2 sts of needle 2, K2tog; SSK at beg of needle 3, knit to last 2 sts of needle 4, K2tog. Work the above 2 rnds 12 times—8 sts on each needle.

Turn mitten inside out and join using three-needle BO method (see page 126).

Thumb: With red, PU the 6 sts from holder, PU another 11 sts around thumb opening—17 sts. Distribute evenly on 3 needles. Knit 18 rnds.

Thumb decs:

Rnd 1: *K1, K2tog*, rep from * to * to last 2 sts, K2.

Rnd 2: Knit.

Rnd 3: *K1, K2tog*, rep from * to *.

Rnd 4: Knit.

Rnd 5: K2tog across rnd. Fasten off.

Cuff: With red and starting at RH side, PU 11 sts to middle of triangle, PU 1 st at middle, PU 11 more sts to LH side. Rep for other triangle. Distribute sts evenly onto 4 needles. Purl 1 rnd, knit 1 rnd, purl 1 rnd. With gray, knit 1 rnd, purl 1 rnd. With black (knit 1 rnd, purl 1 rnd) 2 times, then knit 6 rnds for rolled edge.

BO very loosely in knit.

LEFT MITTEN

Work as for right mitten, but work left thumb as foll:

Left thumb: Work all sts of needle 1, work to last 9 sts of needle 2, place next 6 sts onto holder, CO 6 sts, work last 3 sts of needle.

HAT

With 10" dpn, work beg triangle as for mittens until there are 44 + 1+ 44 sts—89 sts. Join as for mittens, then work rnds 1 and 2 of mitten, foll "Join triangles," for a total of 18 rnds. Work rnds 1 and 2 of "Shape top" for a total of 18 rnds. Join using three-needle BO (see page 126).

Finishing: With black and starting at RH side of lower edge, PU 24 sts to middle of triangle, 1 st in middle of triangle, and 24 more sts to other side of triangle. Rep for second triangle—98 sts. Distribute sts evenly onto 4 needles. Knit 6 rnds for rolled edge. BO very loosely.

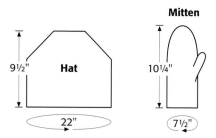

Ice Blue Shell

Alpaca and silk is a combination that few fiber fanatics can ignore. The alpaca imparts the softness; the silk gives it a wonderful luster. Together, it makes for a yarn that you will not want to put down!

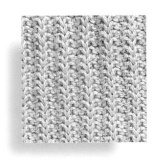

MATERIALS

- 5 (6, 6, 7) skeins Alpaca and Silk from Blue Sky Alpacas (50% superfine alpaca, 50% silk; 50 grams, 146 yards per skein), color Ice Blue #1314, or other sport-weight yarn
- Size 3 (3.25 mm) circular needle (29") or size needed to obtain gauge
- Size 3 (3.25 mm) circular needle (16")
- Size E/4 (3.50 mm) crochet hook
- Stitch holders
- Stitch marker

GAUGE

30 sts and 46 rows = 4" in pattern stitch on size 3 needles

NOTE: The gauge is quite subjective, depending on how much you wish to stretch the piece. The above gauge was taken with the piece lying flat and totally unstretched. Choose your size as to how formfitting you want it to be.

FINISHED MEASUREMENTS

BUST: 29 (31, 33, 35)"*
CENTER BACK LENGTH: 21 (21½, 22½, 23)"

*The lateral stretch of the fabric is very generous. The above measurements will fit actual bust measurements of 34 (36, 38, 40)".

PATTERN STITCH

Multiple of 4 plus 1
Row 1 (WS): K2, *sl 1 wyif, K3*, rep from * to * to last 3 sts, sl 1 wyif, K2.
Row 2 (RS): K4, *sl 1 wyif, K3*, rep from * to * to last st, K1.

FRONT

- Using crochet-chain cast on (see page 126) and 29" needle, CO 109 (117, 125, 133) sts. Work in patt, *dec* 1 st at each side every 1 (1, 1½, 1½)" 3 times, then *inc* 1 st at each side every 1 (1, 1½, 1½)" 3 times.
- Work even until entire piece measures 13½ (14, 14½, 15)", ending with a completed WS row.
- **Shape armholes:** BO 9 sts at beg of next 2 rows. Beg on next row, dec 1 st at each side every 5 rows 7 (7, 8, 9) times—77 (85, 91, 97) sts.
- Work even until entire piece measures 19 (19, 19½, 19½)", ending with a completed WS row.
- **Shape neck:** Work 30 (34, 36, 38) sts, place middle 17 (17, 19, 21) sts on holder for front neck, attach another ball of yarn, and work rem 30 (34, 36, 38) sts. Work each side separately.
- **Right side:** Work 1 row. BO 2 sts at beg of next row (at neck edge). Work 1 row. BO 2 sts at beg of next row. Work 1 row, then dec 1 st at neck edge on next row, then EOR 4 (4, 5, 7) more times—21 (25, 26, 26) sts.
- **Shoulders:** At beg of next 3 RS rows, BO as foll: 7 (8, 9, 9) sts, 7 (8, 9, 9) sts, 7 (9, 8, 8) sts.
- **Left side:** Work as for right side, but beg shaping on first row at neck edge (WS). When neck decs are completed, work 1 row even. BO for shoulders as for right side.

Back

- Work as for front, disregarding neck shaping, until entire piece measures 19¾ (20¼, 20¾, 21¼)" (it should be 4 rows less than beg of shoulder shaping), ending with a completed WS row.
- **Shape back neck:** Work 23 (27, 28, 28) sts, place middle 31 (31, 35, 41) sts on holder for back neck, attach a new ball of yarn, work rem 23 (27, 28, 28) sts. Work each side separately.
- **Left side:** Work WS row, then dec 1 st at neck edge every RS row 2 times. BO for shoulders as for front.
- **Right side:** Work as for left side but beg shaping on WS row.

Finishing

- Sew shoulder and side seams.
- **Neck border:** With RS facing, 16" needle, and beg at left shoulder, PU 8 (8, 10, 10) sts down right back, K31 (31, 35, 41) sts from back neck holder, PU 8 (8, 10, 10) sts up left side of back, K15 (15, 17, 17) sts down left front, K17 (17, 19, 21) sts from front neck holder, PU 15 (15, 17, 17) sts up right front, pm—94 (94, 108, 116) sts. Purl 4 rnds. BO very loosely.
- **Armhole border:** With 16" needle and beg at underarm, PU 47 (47, 51, 51) sts to shoulder seam, PU another 47 (47, 51, 51) sts to underarm, pm—94 (94, 102, 102) sts. Purl 4 rnds. BO very loosely.

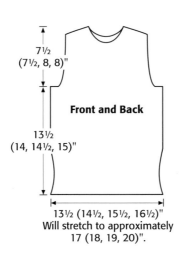

7½ (7½, 8, 8)"

Front and Back

13½ (14, 14½, 15)"

13½ (14½, 15½, 16½)"
Will stretch to approximately
17 (18, 19, 20)".

Heavenly Blue Cardigan

WORKING WITH THIS
yarn is going to be one
of the most wonderful
experiences of your knitting
life! The interesting little
pattern is easily memorized,
letting you savor the knitting. The resulting garment
looks beautiful with either
jeans or black velvet.

MATERIALS

- 8 (9, 10) skeins Heaven Sent from Haneke (70% baby royal alpaca, 30% wool; 50 grams, 200 yards per skein), color Denim Blue, or other sport-weight yarn
- Size 4 (3.5 mm) straight needles
- Size 4 (3.5 mm) circular needle (16")
- Size 5 (3.75 mm) needles or size needed to obtain gauge
- Cable needle
- 5 (4, 6) buttons, ⅝" diameter

GAUGE

26½ sts and 32 rows = 4" in cable and lace pattern on size 5 needles

FINISHED MEASUREMENTS

BUST: 38 (44½, 50)"
CENTER BACK LENGTH: 20¾ (22¼, 23¾)"

PATTERN STITCHES

Border Pattern

Multiple of 10 plus 4
NOTE: Sl all sts pw wyif on WS of work.

Row 1 (RS): K3, *P8, K2*, rep from * to * to last st, K1.

Row 2 (WS): Sl 3, *K8, sl 2*, rep from * to * to last st, sl 1.

Row 3: K1, *K2, P1, K6, P1*, rep from * to * to last 3 sts, K3.

Row 4: Sl 3, *K1, P6, K1, sl 2*, rep from * to * to last st, sl 1.

Cable and Lace Pattern

Multiple of 10 plus 6
NOTE: Sl all sts kw wyib on WS of work.

Row 1 (RS): K4, *P2, K4, P2, K2tog, YO*, rep from * to * to last 12 sts, P2, K4, P2, K4.

Row 2 (WS): P4, *K2, P4, K2, P2*, rep from * to * to last 12 sts, K2, P4, K2, P4.

Row 3: K4, *P2, C4F, P2, YO, sl 1, K1, psso*, rep from * to * to last 12 sts, P2, C4F, P2, K4.

Row 4: As row 2.

Row 5: As row 1.

Row 6: As row 2.

Row 7: K4, *P2, K4, P2, YO, sl 1, K1, psso*, rep from * to * to last 12 sts, P2, K4, P2, K4.

Row 8: As row 2.

BACK

NOTE: This pattern stitch is composed of an eight-stitch cable on the right side (P2, K4, P2), followed by 2 stitches that form the lace (K2tog, YO, or sl 1, K2, psso). Wrong-side rows correspond as cable (K2, P4, K2) and lace (P2). The two stitches of the lace make a hole that is not desirable close to any edge (armhole edge) or shoulder seam. Therefore, do not work the two stitches of the lace pattern between the cables any closer than four stitches from an edge while working decreases.

- With size 4 straight needles, CO 124 (144, 164) sts. Work 4 rows of border patt 11 times.
- **Next 2 rows:** CO 1 st, purl to end of row; CO 1 st, knit to end of row—126 (146, 166) sts.
- Change to size 5 (3.75 mm) needles and work 8 rows of cable and lace pattern 8 (9, 10) times.
- **Shape armholes:** (NOTE: Do not work the 2 sts of the lace patt between the cables any closer than 4 sts from edge while working decs.) BO 10 (12, 14) sts at beg of next 2 rows—106 (122, 138) sts. Dec 1 st at each side every RS row 8 (10, 12) times—90 (102, 114) sts. Work WS row.
- Work even for 48 (56, 60) rows, ending with a completed WS row. (NOTE: For size 44½ only: Do not work 2-st lace patt at very edge of armhole, but instead work these 2 sts as St st.)

- **Next row (RS):** Work 27 (31, 35) sts, work middle 36 (40, 44) sts and place on holder for back neck, work rem 27 (31, 35) sts. Work each side separately.
- **Short-row shoulder and neck shaping (left side):** Work WS row.
  Row 1 (RS): Dec 1 st at neck edge, work 15 (17, 19) more sts, W and T.
  Row 2: Work back.
  Row 3: Dec 1 st at neck edge, work 6 (8, 9) more sts, hiding wrap from row 1, W and T.
  Row 4: Work back.
  Row 5: Dec 1 st at neck edge, work across row, hiding wraps from rows 1 and 3. Work 2-st lace patt for this row as K2. Place rem 24 (28, 32) sts on holder.
- **Right side:** Attach yarn at neck edge on WS and work rows 1–5 as for left side, then work 1 row in St st. Place rem 24 (28, 32) sts on holder.

LEFT FRONT

- With size 4 straight needles, CO 64 (74, 84) sts. Work border as for back.
- **Next 2 rows:** CO 1 st, purl to end of row. CO 1 st, knit to end of row—66 (76, 86) sts.
- Change to size 5 needles and work cable and lace patt as for back, crossing cable as C4B and working armhole on RH side of piece. After armhole shaping is completed, 48 (54, 60) sts rem, and WS row has been worked, work 33 (39, 41) more rows.
- **Shape neck:** Work first 17 (18, 19) sts and place on holder for front neck, work to end of row. Starting next row, dec 1 st at neck edge every WS row 7 (8, 9) times—24 (28, 32) sts.
- Work RS row, then work short-row shoulder shaping as foll:
  Row 1: Work 16 (18, 20) sts, W and T.
  Row 2: Work back.
  Row 3: Work 7 (9, 10) sts, W and T.
  Row 4: Work back.

Row 5: Work across row, hiding wraps from rows 1 and 3.

RIGHT FRONT

Work as for left front, but cross cables as C4F and reverse all shaping. Work 32 (38, 40) more rows after armhole shaping has been completed, then beg neck shaping on next row (RS). When neck shaping has been completed, work WS row, then beg short-row shoulder shaping as for left front.

SEAMING AND NECK

- **Join shoulders:** Use three-needle BO (see page 126), dec 1 st over each cable as you BO.
- **Neck:** With size 4 circ needle and starting at right front, knit 17 (18, 19) sts from front neck holder, dec 1 st over each cable, PU 15 (17, 19) sts up to shoulder, PU 5 sts down right back, knit sts from back neck holder, dec 1 st over each cable, PU 5 sts up left back, PU 15 (17, 19) sts down left front, knit 17 (18, 19) sts from left front holder. *Turn work and knit WS, turn work and purl RS*, rep from * to * 3 times. BO very loosely.

FRONT BANDS

- **Left band:** With size 4 straight needles and starting at neck edge PU 94 (104, 114) sts. Go through both thicknesses of rolled neck edge, then PU about 3 sts for every 4 sts down front, ending at purl ridge that separates border of sweater from main body. Work foll 4 rows 2 times, then work rows 1 and 2 again for a total of 10 rows.
  Row (WS): Sl 3, *K8, sl 2*, rep from * to * to last st, sl 1.
  Row 2 (RS): K3, *P8, K2*, rep from * to * to last st, K1.
  Row 3: Sl 3, *K1, P6, K1, sl 2*, rep from * to * to last st, sl 1.

Row 4: K3, *P1, K6, P1, K2*, rep from * to * to last st, K1. BO from WS very loosely in knit.

- **Right band:** Work as for left band, but beg at lower edge of sweater. Work 5 rows, then work 5 buttonholes in every other section for size Small, 4 buttonholes in every third section for size Medium, and 6 buttonholes in every other section for size Large. Buttonholes are worked on the RS as follows:

  Step 1: K3, P2, wyif sl the next st pw, place yarn in back and *sl 1 pw, pass previous st over it* rep from * to * until 4 sts have been bound off. Sl last BO st to LH needle and turn work. Yarn is in back.

  Step 2: Cable-edge cast on 4 sts, then cable-edge cast on 1 more st, but put yarn in front before placing this last st on needle. Turn work.

  Step 3: Sl 1 st kw and pass extra cast-on st over it. Work last sts of section to K2 line of sts.

  Step 4: Work next buttonholes as above, but beg in appropriate section of band after K2, P2.

- Finish right band as for left band.
- Sew buttons on left band.

SLEEVES

- With size 4 straight needles, CO 60 (70, 80) sts. Work border pattern for sleeve as foll:

Row 1: P4, *K2, P8*, rep from * to * to last 6 sts, K2, P4.

Row 2: K4, *sl 2, K8*, rep from * to * to last 6 sts, sl 2, P4.

Row 3: K3, P1, *K2, P1, K6, P1*, rep from * to * to last 6 sts, K2, P1, K3.

Row 4: P3, K1, * sl 2, K1, P6, K1*, rep from * to * to last 6 sts, sl 2, K1, P3.

Rows 5 and 6: Purl.

- Change to size 5 needles, then work cable and lace setup row as foll:
- K2, P2, *K2tog, YO, P2, K4, P2*, rep from * to * to last 6 sts, K2tog, YO, P2, K2.
- Cont in established patt, inc 1 st at each side every 4 rows 25 (28, 26) times, then every 3 rows 3 (0, 0) times—116 (126, 132) sts. Work 3 (4, 16) rows even.

  NOTE: Incorporate new sts into existing patt, but do not work 2-st lace patt any closer than 2 sts from each edge.

- **Shape cap:** BO 10 (12, 14) sts at beg of next 2 rows—96 (102, 104) sts. Dec 1 st at each side every RS row 12 (14, 16) times—72 (74, 72) sts. Work WS row, then BO 2 sts at beg of next 12 rows. BO rem 48 (50, 48) sts, dec 1 st over each cable during BO.

FINISHING

- Sew sleeves into armholes.
- Sew side seams just to border.
- Sew sleeve seams.
- Sew buttons to left front.

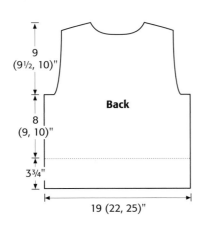

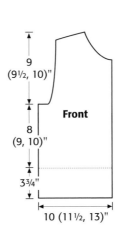

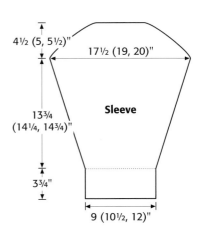

Llama Cables

LLAMA FIBER IS incredibly soft and fluffy, but has very little memory. Combining it with wool gives it the memory it needs for it to stretch and then go back to its original shape. This sweater is worked in a basic rib pattern with allover cables, making it form-fitting but stretchy and comfortable. The funnel neck adds practical warmth without being restrictive. I think this is the perfect sweater—with regards to color, ease, and warmth—to wear while raking leaves on a chilly autumn day.

MATERIALS

- 8 (9, 10) skeins Pastaza from Cascade Yarns (50% llama, 50% wool; 100 grams, 132 yards per skein), color Rust #62, or other worsted-weight yarn
- Size 9 (5.5 mm) needles or size needed to obtain gauge
- Size 10 (6 mm) needles
- One set of 7"-long double-pointed needles, size 9 (5.5 mm)
- Cable needle
- Stitch markers
- Stitch holders

FINISHED MEASUREMENTS

BUST: 35 (41, 47)"
TOTAL BACK LENGTH INCLUDING FUNNEL
     NECK: 25¼ (27¾, 30½)"

GAUGE

25¾ sts and 21 rows = 4" in pattern stitch on size 9 needles

NOTE: These figures are the actual measurement of the unstretched cables. When worn, there is a lateral stretch of 6" or more.

PATTERN STITCH

Cable Column (CbCl)

Work over 11 sts as follows: (K2, P1) 3 times, K2.

The patt is 40 rows, with cables being turned on alternating columns on rows 5, 15, 25, and 35 as foll: Sl 5 sts to cn and hold in front, (K2, P1) 2 times from LH needle, K2, P1, K2 from cn.

NOTE: Do not turn cables unless you have the full 11 sts to work with, such as in armhole and neck shaping.

BACK AND FRONT

- With size 10 needles, CO 103 (115, 127) sts. Change to size 9 needles.
- **Row 1:**
  Small: K3, (P1, K2) 2 times, P1, CbCl#1, P1, CbCl#2, P1, CbCl#3, P1, CbCl#4, P1, CbCl#5, P1, CbCl#6, P1, CbCl#7, P1, (K2, P1) 2 times, K3.
  Medium: K3, P1, CbCl#1, P1, CbCl#2, P1, CbCl#3, P1, CbCl#4, P1, CbCl#5, P1, CbCl#6, P1, CbCl#7, P1, CbCl#8, P1, CbCl#9, P1, K3.
  Large: K3, (P1, K2) 2 times, P1, CbCl#1, P1, CbCl#2, P1, CbCl#3, P1, CbCl#4, P1, CbCl#5, P1, CbCl#6, P1, CbCl#7, P1, CbCl#8, P1, CbCl#9, P1, (K2, P1) 2 times, K3.
- **Row 2 and all WS rows for all sizes:** Knit the knit sts and purl the purl sts.
- Work above patt, turning cables for size small on CbCl#s 1, 3, 5, and 7 on rows 5 and 15, and on CbCl#s 2, 4, and 6 on rows 25 and 35. Turn cables for sizes Medium and Large on CbCl#s 1, 3, 5, 7, and 9 on rows 5 and 15, and CbCl#s 2, 4, 6, and 8 on rows 25 and 35. The patt is a 40-row rep. Work 80 (90, 100) rows of patt.
- **Shape armholes:** BO 7 (9, 11) sts at beg of next 2 rows, dec 1 st at each side every RS row 6 (8, 10) times—77 (81, 85) sts and 13 (17, 21) rows.
- Work 29 rows, marking off center 31 (31, 37) sts on last row with markers—42 (46, 50) rows total from beg of armhole shaping.
- **Shape shoulders and neck:**
  Row 1 (RS): Work to 2 sts before marker, K2tog, work center sts, SSK, work to end of row.
  Row 2: Work to end of row, working sts that were worked tog as purl sts.
  Row 3: BO 7 sts, work to 2 sts before marker, K2tog, work center sts, SSK, work to end of row.

Row 4: BO 7 sts, work as for row 2.

Row 5: BO 7 sts, work to 2 sts before marker, K2tog, work center sts, SSK, work to end of row.

Row 6: BO 7 sts, work as for row 2.

Row 7: BO 5 (7, 6) sts, work to end of row.

Row 8: BO 5 (7, 6) sts, work to end of row—1 st left on needle on each side, plus 31 (31, 37) center sts. Place these 33 (33, 39) sts on holder for funnel neck.

SLEEVES

- With size 10 needle, CO 39 (47, 63) sts. Change to size 9 needles.
- **Row 1:**
  Small: K1, P1, CbCl#1, P1, CbCl#2, P1, CbCl#3, P1, K1. Turn CbCl#2 on rows 5 and 15, and CbCl#1 and CbCl#3 on rows 25 and 35.
  Medium: (K2, P1) 2 times, CbCl#1, P1, CbCl#2, P1, CbCl#3, (P1, K2) 2 times. Turn CbCl#2 on rows 5 and 15, and CbCl#1 and CbCl#3 on rows 25 and 35.
  Large: K1, P1, CbCl#1, P1, CbCl#2, P1, CbCl#3, P1, CbCl#4, P1, CbCl#5, P1, K1. Turn CbCl#s 1, 3, and 5 on rows 5 and 15, and CbCl#2 and CbCl#4 on rows 25 and 35.

- Work in patt, inc 1 st at each side every 7 rows 13 (13, 14) times—65 (73, 91) sts. Extra sts on sides are worked into K2, P1 patt.
- Work even through row 16 (16, 20) of patt.
- **Cap shaping:** Do not turn CbCl#1 and CbCl#3 anymore. BO 7 (9, 11) sts at beg of next 2 rows, dec 1 st at each side every RS row 6 (8, 10) times—39 (39, 49) sts. Work 3 rows even.
- **BO as foll:** 1 st at beg of next 2 rows, 2 sts at beg of next 4 rows. BO rem 29 (29, 39) sts.

FINISHING

- Sew shoulder seams.
- **Neck:** With size 9 dpn and starting at shoulder, work sts on holders in patt as foll:
- K1, P1, *K2, P1*, rep from * to * to last st, K1—33 (33, 39) sts each for front and back—total 66 (66, 78) sts. Work 10 rnds. BO very loosely in knit.
- Sew side seams of body.
- Sew sleeve seams; sew sleeves into armholes.
- Do not press directly on cables with steam iron, but hover iron over cables and press steam button.

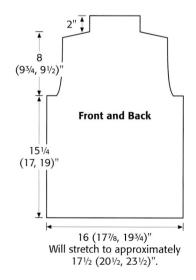

Front and Back

2"

8 (9¾, 9½)"

15¼ (17, 19)"

16 (17⅞, 19¾)"
Will stretch to approximately 17½ (20½, 23½)".

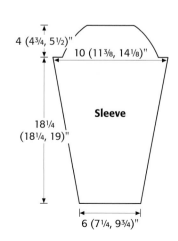

Sleeve

4 (4¾, 5½)"

10 (11⅜, 14⅛)"

18¼ (18¼, 19)"

6 (7¼, 9¾)"

Cashmere

Cashmere Goat (Photo by Marilyn Ackley)

*I*F CASHMERE WERE a sound, it would be the seductive whisper of a lover; if it were a violin, it would be a Stradivarius; if it were an emotion, it would be love. Light as a feather and softer than words can describe, a garment knit from cashmere floats on your body, offering luxurious caresses wherever it touches bare skin. Knitters everywhere worship its very existence, but take a look at the animal from which it comes. Cashmere goats probably originated in the region of India known as Kashmir, a land that offers very little food and natural shelter from severely cold and windy weather. In order to survive in such a climate, the goats developed a warm, lightweight undercoat. Over it, exposed to the elements, is a long and shaggy coat of coarse guard hair.

It's hard to imagine that the very silky and expensive skein of yarn you just coveted in the yarn store could actually come from such an animal! But ruffle up the guard hair, and there it is—that silken undercoat that is the humble beginnings of that expensive skein. Color variety of the goats ranges from pure white to various hues of grays and browns.

According to legend, the first cashmere goats in this country were brought to Texas by the Spanish and used for meat and milk. As the Spanish gradually disappeared from that part of the country, the remaining goats went feral. Texas cattle ranchers gunned down the goats in huge numbers, viewing them as a nuisance for grazing on the land used for cattle. It is possible that no one knew of the fiber possibilities these animals possessed, but it is also just as likely that they were aware of it but not interested. It was easier to get fiber from sheep. The cashmere goats that are in this country now are not a breed, per se, but have all been genetically bred for fine fiber from these wild goats.

In order for the fiber to be considered cashmere, it must have a micron count of 18½ or lower, and a minimum fiber length of 1¼". The more crimp the fiber possesses, the softer and warmer it is. In order to get a very fine fiber from just controlling an animal's environment, the animal has to be close to starvation. Of course, this is not an option, because the goat would likely die before the fiber could be obtained. Instead, careful genetics are used to breed goats for fine fiber quality. There is a point, however, where the fineness of the fiber must be considered for economic reasons. The finer the fiber, the less it weighs, and it would be very hard to breed enough goats to make any money.

Each goat produces only about 4 to 6 ounces of cashmere per year, which is obtained by either shearing or hand combing. Most of the Western world shears; most of the Eastern world hand combs. Shearing can be done anytime the fleece has grown to its fullest, but combing can be done only for a few weeks each spring when the hair follicles of the goat release. Guard hairs, which account for as much as 80% of the fleece, must be separated from the soft underfleece. Before the advent of modern machinery, this tedious job was accomplished by hand. Having no use, the guard hair is thrown out. The fiber then goes through much the same process as wool: washing, carding, spinning, and plying. China and Mongolia are responsible for producing 75% of the world's cashmere. The remaining 25% comes from Iran, Afghanistan, Turkey, Pakistan, Australia, New Zealand, India, and the United States.

Yvonne Taylor, Wendy Pieh, and Marilyn Ackley, three cashmere goat farmers from Maine, gathered together at Yvonne's Maine farm on a snowy day in December to talk with me about all things cashmere. As we started talking, I sensed immediately that these three women were in mutual agreement that cashmere goats were the best thing that ever happened to them, although at the time they acquired them, fine fiber was the furthest thing from their minds! All three women initially bought goats to help them clear their land. It seems that goats will eat almost anything, and clear the land they did.

The three women good naturedly banter about their opinionated positions on whether to shear or comb. Marilyn advocates shearing, the biggest advantage being "it gets the job done." Hand combing can sometimes take several days—perhaps about 30 minutes spent per day—and it involves synchronizing the human schedule of one's life with the shedding schedule of individual goats. Marilyn also claims that shearing preserves

Cashmere Does at Rabbit Tree Farm

(Photo by Paul C. Merbach)

the integrity of the cashmere. By combing the delicate down through the long and rough guard hairs, there is the possibility of damage. But combers say the shorn goats can get cold. Marilyn's solution, since she was a costume designer before she became a goat farmer, is her little goat coats that are an ingenious combination of design and function: a weather resistant outer layer, a warm wool lining, and nice little fastenings. When clothed, the goats sport the chic and classic good looks of little bankers in pinstriped suits!

Yvonne and Wendy, however, prefer to hand comb, maintaining that shearing loses some of the weight of the fleece, since about ¼" is left on the body. With their guard hair still intact, they eat less in order to keep warm than their chilly cousins who have been shorn. (But Marilyn counteracts this by dressing them as bankers!) The fiber gets dehaired in fewer passes when put through the machine, reducing the chance of damage, and Yvonne says that combing puts less stress on an animal, plus you do not have a sharp end on the fibers from cutting. It is true that the people who hand comb are in a minority in this world of technology and electricity, but as Yvonne says, "Combing is a poetic, lyrical activity and an excuse to hang out with the goats."

For cashmere to be at its softest, it must possess no more than ½% of guard hair. This dehairing process is pretty much a closely guarded secret, but Wendy has recently purchased a spinning mill and she briefly explained the process to me. The dehairing equipment is about 100 feet in length and has eight rollers. The first pass of the fiber through the machinery rids the fleece of about 90% of its guard hair. The trick is to get most of the guard hair out without putting it through too many times, as each time it goes through the rollers, the chances of damaging the fragile fibers increase.

The Cashmere Cooperative of America processes and sells American cashmere, providing a much needed service for small farmers who don't have a large-enough yield to sell to a big mill. The coop buys the raw fleece from each farmer, and any profits, once it has been processed and sold, is divided among the members.

With the popularity of cashmere on the rise, the demand is almost greater than the supply. Drought conditions in China and Mongolia over the last several years have greatly reduced the number of goats. And what about this marvelous stuff out there called pashmina that every knitter wants but can't afford? According to some sources, pashmina is the highest-quality cashmere that comes only from the neck and belly of the goat. According to other sources, pashmina is just cashmere and is not necessarily any softer or of better quality. In the American and European market, the term pashmina is not even recognized as a fiber description.

Faced with all the choices, what should the smart knitter look for in a skein of cashmere? Trust your hands. Feel the yarn, then look at it closely. If you can see lots of guard hairs, then it probably is not the softest it could be. Feel a skein of dyed yarn and then compare it to a skein of undyed. Some dyeing processes can make the fiber less soft, while others do nothing at all to change it. Don't shun a beautiful skein because it is a blend. Cashmere blended with silk is a delight, with the silk contributing luster and strength. Add merino to cashmere and you get more fluff without added weight.

When I first entered Yvonne's living room to talk, Wendy handed me three skeins of the softest yarn I ever felt. Hand spun from her own goats, she admitted that it wasn't even her finest fiber. Throughout our time together, I kept reaching for those skeins to fondle, and when it was time to finally leave, I had a hard time walking away from them. I was seduced.

KNITTING AND DESIGNING WITH CASHMERE

IN deciding what kind of garment to make with the cashmere, I basically had two things to consider. This wonderful fiber, alas, is very expensive. Most cashmere, however, is spun very thin, yielding a lot of yardage in relation to the weight. My second deciding factor was that I wanted the wearer to really know they were wearing cashmere.

The hand of Mountain Colors Ruby River 100% cashmere was so soft, so sensual, that I decided it had to be against the skin. I therefore designed the hooded scarf, and with the leftovers, made mittens (page 44).

A simple lace pattern adds elegance to this hooded scarf.

Picot trim adds a delicate border to this lace pattern in the Cornflower Cardigan.

When I designed the Razor Shell Shawl (page 47) with Rabbit Tree Hill 100% cashmere, I envisioned a romantic and gossamer covering to wear over bare arms on a balmy summer night. I also wanted something so simple that the knitter would not have to constantly refer to directions, thus taking away from the supreme pleasure of just knitting with this stuff.

Traditional Shetland Lace Pattern of Razor Shell Done in Garter Stitch

Thinking nothing could be softer than 100% cashmere, was I ever surprised when I started swatching with the K1C2 Richesse et Soie, which is 65% cashmere and 35% silk! This yarn had all the softness of cashmere with just a slight sheen that the silk added. I heard the seductive whispering of "lace," and the Cornflower Cardigan (page 50) was conceived. I chose a German pattern, elegant but very simple to knit.

Don't be fooled about the size 3 needles. I couldn't believe how fast this knit up. Maybe because it was such a sheer joy to be holding the yarn! Next time you are in a yarn store, succumb to the seductive whisper; you won't be sorry. Beaded Pulse Warmers (page 54), which echo the lace design of the sweater, complete the ensemble.

Beading is a simple way to add pattern to any project.

Hooded Scarf and Mittens

DO NOT BE DAUNTED by the number of stitches you are working on. The whole point of cashmere is to knit with it! The more stitches, the more knitting; the more knitting, the more pleasure. Enjoy!

Materials for Scarf and Mittens

- 5 skeins 100% Superfine Cashmere from Mountain Colors (100% cashmere; 28 grams, 95 yards per skein), color Ruby River, or other sport-weight yarn
- Size 5 (3.75 mm) circular needle (29") or size needed to obtain gauge for scarf
- One set of double-pointed needles, size 5 (3.75 mm) or size needed to obtain gauge for mittens
- Stitch marker

Gauge

26 sts and 32 rows = 4" in stockinette stitch on size 5 needles

Finished Measurements

Scarf ends (minus hood) each 21" long, 5" wide

Note: If you wish to make the scarf ends of this hat longer, simply cast on more stitches in a multiple of 5. Keep the middle 120 sts for the shaped hood, working the tie ends exactly the same but on more stitches. You can also substitute any of your favorite lace patterns, or even work it in a solid pattern.

Small (Large) Mitten Length: 10½ (11)"
Small (Large) Mitten Circumference: 13 (15)"

Pattern Stitch for Scarf

Row 1 (RS): K1, P1, K1, P1, *K3, YO, K2tog*, rep from * to * to last 7 sts, K3, P1, K1, P1, K1.

Row 2 (WS): K1, P1, K1, P1, *P4, K1*, rep from * to * to last 7 sts, P3, P1, K1, P1, K1.

Row 3: K1, P1, K1, P1, *K3, K2tog, YO*, rep from * to * to last 7 sts, K3, P1, K1, P1, K1.

Row 4: K1, P1, K1, P1, P3, *K1, P4 *, rep from * to * to last 4 sts, P1, K1, P1, K1.
Rep rows 1–4 for patt.

Pattern Stitch for Mittens

- **Rnd 1 (RS):** *K3, YO, K2tog *, rep from * to *.
- **Rnd 2 (WS):** *P1, K4 *, rep from * to *.
- **Rnd 3:** *K3, K2tog, YO *, rep from * to *. Note: Remember to YO at end of round.
- **Rnd 4:** *K4, P1*, rep from * to *.

Scarf

- CO 371 sts. Work rev St st for rolled hem as foll:
  Row 1 (RS): Purl.
  Row 2 (WS): Knit.
  Rep these 2 rows 3 times—6 rows total.
- Work the 4 rows of patt 11 times—44 rows total.
- Work rev St st for rolled hem on first 126 sts. BO.
- Put middle 120 sts onto holder. Attach yarn and work rev St st for rolled hem on last 125 sts. BO.
- Place middle 120 sts on needle and attach yarn. Work head shaping on middle 120 sts as foll:
  Row 1 (RS): K62, wyib sl 1 kw, K1, psso, K1. Turn work.
  Row 2 (WS): Wyif sl 1 pw, P5, P2tog, P1. Turn work.
  Row 3: Wyib sl 1 pw, knit to within 1 st of gap, wyib sl 1 kw, K1, psso, K1. Turn work.
  Row 4: Wyif sl 1 pw, purl to within 1 st of gap, P2tog, P1. Turn work.
  Rep rows 3 and 4 until all sts are used up, ending with a completed WS row—62 sts.
- Work rev St st for rolled hem, dec 10 sts evenly spaced across first row—52 sts. BO.

FINISHING

- Sew two tiny seams between scarf ends and bottom of head shaping.

Hooded Scarf

Mittens

Want to feel the luxury of cashmere on your hands even when you're not knitting with it? Knit these elegant mittens, and then wear them!

CUFF

- Very loosely CO 40 (50) sts. Sl equal number of sts to 4 dpn, join rnd, pm. Purl 6 rnds.
- Work in patt for 3".
- Knit 1 rnd, inc 2 (dec 2) sts evenly spaced—42 (48) sts.

HAND

- Working in St st (knit every rnd), knit 4 rnds.
- **First inc for thumb gore:** K1, pm, inc 1 st st (M1R) in second st of round (first st of thumb gore), K1, inc 1 st (M1L) in next st (last st of thumb gore), pm, knit to end of rnd—44 (50) sts. Thumb gore is bordered by markers.

- Knit 2 rnds even.
- **Second inc for thumb gore:** Inc 1 st in first st of thumb gore, K3, inc in next st, knit to end of rnd—46 (52) sts.
- Cont to inc 1 st in first and last st of thumb gore every 3 rnds 5 (6) more times—56 (64) sts. Knit 2 rnds even.
- K1, sl 15 (17) thumb sts to a thread, CO 3 sts, work to end of rnd—44 (50) sts.
- Work even until 6½ (6¾)" from top of cuff. Work 1 rnd, dec 2 (0) sts evenly spaced—42 (50) sts.
- **First dec rnd:** (K2, K2tog) 10 (12) times—32 (38) sts.
- Knit 3 (4) rnds even.
- **Second dec rnd:** (K1, K2tog) 10 (12) times—22 (26) sts.
- Knit 3 (4) rnds even.
- **Third dec rnd:** K2tog 10 (12) times around—12 (14) sts.
- Break yarn and fasten off by drawing yarn through all sts.

THUMB

- Divide the 15 (17) thumb sts onto 2 needles. With a third needle, PU 4 sts into the CO stitches—19 (21) sts.
- Knit 1 rnd, dec 1 st over CO sts—18 (20) sts.
- Knit until thumb measures 2 (2½)", dec 0 (2) sts evenly spaced on last rnd—18 (18) sts.
- **First dec rnd:** *K1, K2tog*, rep from * to *.
- Knit 2 rnds even.
- **Second dec rnd:** K2tog across rnd.
- Fasten off as for hand.

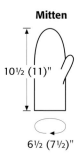

Mitten

10½ (11)"

6½ (7½)"

Razor Shell Shawl

SIMPLY CONSTRUCTED in a very easy and traditional Shetland lace pattern, this shawl starts at one tip, and increases are worked every wrong-side row, with one additional increase every three rows. This makes the horizontal measurement grow at the same rate as the vertical measurement, yielding an isosceles right triangle. The shawl is worn with the hypotenuse over the shoulders. A ruffled edging done in garter stitch is worked directly onto picked-up stitches, with a crochet bind off finishing everything off.

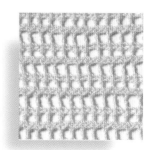

Materials

- 5 skeins 100% 2-ply Cashmere from Rabbit Tree Farm (28 grams, 200 yards per skein), color Natural White, or other fingering-weight yarn
- Size 7 (4.5 mm) circular needle (29") or size needed to obtain gauge
- Size E/4 (3.5 mm) crochet hook
- Stitch markers

Gauge (after blocking)

Approximately 20 sts and 28 rows = 4" in pattern stitch on size 7 needles

Finished Measurements (after blocking)

Center Back Length: 33"

Shawl

- CO 3 sts.
  Row 1: Knit.
  Row 2: YO, knit to last st, wyif sl last st pw. Rep these 2 rows until there are 7 sts.
- **Beg pattern stitch:**
  Row 1 (RS): K3 sts for border, *YO, sl 1 wyib, K2tog, psso, YO, K1*, rep from * to *.
  Row 2: YO, knit to last st, wyif sl last st pw.
  Row 3 and all odd rows: Work as for row 1, but work last 1, 2, or 3 sts after last rep as knit. On rows that have a multiple of 4 within lace patt (after 3 sts of border), knit into front and back of last st. This will make one extra st on RS row every 3 rows.
  Row 4: As row 2.
  Rep rows 3 and 4 until there are 199 sts on needle, ending with a completed row 4.

- Work foll 4 rows:
  Row 1: Knit.
  Row 2: YO, knit to end of row.
  Rows 3 and 4: Knit.
- BO as foll: K2, *pass first st over second st but leave on left needle. Knit next st, then sl both sts off tog*, rep from * to *.
- **PU for edging:** PU 1 st for every sl st on side A (151 sts), pm, PU 1 st at point, pm, PU 1 st for every BO st on side B (193 sts)—total 345 sts.
  NOTE: If you do not get exactly 345 sts, merely adjust on foll row to get correct number for patt rep.
- **Next row:** Knit, dec 43 sts evenly spaced along side B (150 sts), knit point st, knit sts of side A, dec 1 st (150 sts)—total 301 sts.
- **Eyelet row:** *K2tog, YO*, rep from * to * to point st, knit point st, **YO, K2tog**, rep from ** to ** to end of row. Knit 1 row.
- **Ruffle edging (multiple of 4 plus 2):**
  Row 1 (RS): K2, *YO, K1, YO, K3*, rep from * to * to point st, YO, knit point st, YO, **K3, YO, K1, YO**, rep from ** to ** to last 2 sts, K2.
  Row 2 and all even rows (WS): Knit.
  Row 3: K3, *YO, K1, YO, K5*, rep from * to * to point st, YO, knit point st, YO, **K5, YO, K1, YO**, rep from ** to ** to last 3 sts, K3.
  Row 5: K4, *YO, K1, YO, K7*, rep from * to * to point st, YO, knit point st, YO, **K7, YO, K1, YO**, rep from ** to ** to last 4 sts, K4.
  Rows 7, 9, 11, and 13: Cont in above manner, knit 1 more st at beg and end of row, keeping YOs in same place, but knit 2 extra sts between them on each successive row.

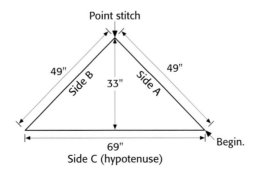

- **Crochet bind off:** Put first st from needle onto crochet hook. *Ch 5, sl next 2 sts pw from needle to crochet hook. Draw thread through all 3 sts on hook*, rep from * to * to point st. Sl point st only onto hook, draw yarn through 2 sts. Cont along other side of shawl as for first side.

Finishing

Wash and block by folding in half to get a perfect triangle. After shawl is dry, run your fingers along the border to spread out ruffling.

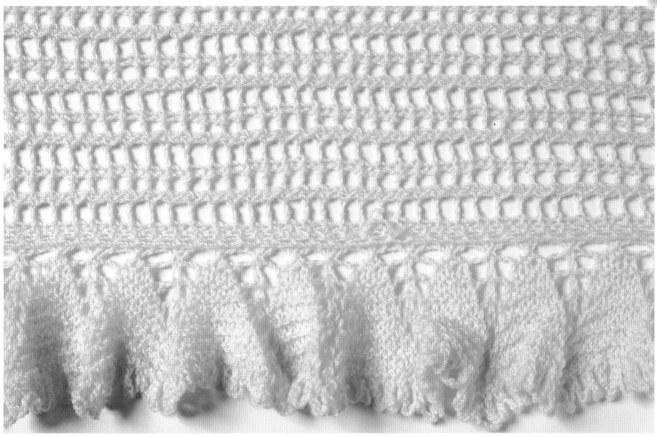

Point stitch

49"   Side B   33"   Side A   49"

69"
Side C (hypotenuse)

Begin.

Cornflower Cardigan

THE SILKY SOFTNESS
of this yarn is a sheer joy,
and the simple lace pattern
puts elegance into this
classic-fitting cardigan.

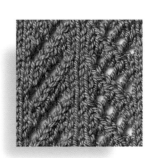

MATERIALS

- 9 (11, 13) skeins Richesse et Soie from K1C2 Gourmet Collection (65% cashmere, 35% silk; 25 grams, 145 yards per skein), color Cornflower Blue, or other sport-weight yarn
- Size 3 (3.25 mm) needles or size needed to obtain gauge
- Size 1 (2.25 mm) circular (29") needle
- Size E/4 (3.50 mm) crochet hook (for CO)
- Size 1 (2.75 mm) steel crochet hook (for picot border)
- 1 small button
- Stitch markers

GAUGE

27 sts and 40 rows = 4" in lace pattern on size 3 needles

FINISHED MEASUREMENTS

BUST: 36 (43½, 51¼)"
CENTER BACK LENGTH: 17¾ (20, 21¾)"

PATTERN STITCH

The pattern stitch for each individual piece is written under the appropriate heading.

NOTE: When working a lace pattern, it is important to remember that a decrease (either a K2tog or an SSK) is always paired with a yarnover. When decreasing or increasing within the pattern, you may not always have enough stitches to work the K2tog or SSK with the corresponding yarnover. In such a case, just work the stitches as stockinette stitch until it is possible to resume the established lace pattern.

RIGHT FRONT

- Using size E/4 crochet hook, size 3 needle, and crochet-chain cast on (see page 126), CO 57 (70, 83) sts. Knit 1 row, purl 1 row. Beg of all odd-numbered rows is center front edge; end of all odd-numbered rows is side edge (where inc is done; see below).
- **Pattern stitch for right front:**
  NOTE: To keep track of where you are in the lace pattern, place markers between each of the 13-st reps.
  Row 1 (RS): K2, *K3, YO, SSK, K5, K2tog, YO, K1*, rep from * to * to last 3 sts, K3.
  Rows 2, 4, and 6: Purl.
  Row 3: K2, *K4, YO, SSK, K3, K2tog, YO, K2*, rep from * to * to last 3 sts, K3.
  Row 5: K2, *K2, YO, SSK, K1, YO, SSK, K1, K2tog, YO, K1, K2tog, YO*, rep from * to * to last 3 sts, K3.
  Work the above 6-row rep a total of 17 (19, 21) times, inc 1 st at side edge on rows 20, 40, 60, 80, and 100, working additional st as St st—62 (75, 88) sts. Work 1 row.
- **Shape armholes:** Keeping at least 5 sts at armhole edge in St st, on WS row, BO 8 (12, 16) sts. Work RS row. Dec 1 st at armhole edge every WS row 8 (12, 16) times—46 (51, 56) sts.
- Work even until armhole measures 5¾ (6¼, 6¾)", ending with a completed WS row.
- **Shape front neck:** On RS row, BO 15 (16, 17) sts. Work 2 rows. Dec 1 st at neck edge, then every 6 rows 2 more times—28 (32, 36) sts.
- Work even until armhole measures 7¼ (8, 8¾)", ending with a completed RS row.
- At beg of next 3 WS rows, BO as foll: 9 (10, 12) sts, 9 (11, 12) sts, and 10 (11, 12) sts. (Work sts that will be bound off on next row in St st.)

Left Front

- CO as for right front. Knit 1 row, purl 1 row. Beg of all odd-numbered rows is side edge (where inc is done; see below); end of all odd-numbered rows is center front edge.
- **Pattern stitch for left front:**
  Row 1: K3, * K1, YO, SSK, K5, K2tog, YO, K3*, rep from * to * to last 2 sts, K2.
  Rows 2, 4, and 6: Purl.
  Row 3: K3, *K2, YO, SSK, K3, K2tog, YO, K4*, rep from * to *to last 2 sts, K2.
  Row 5: K3, *YO, SSK, K1, YO, SSK, K1, K2tog, YO, K1, K2tog, YO, K2*, rep from * to * to last 2 sts, K2.
  Work in above patt as for right front, reversing all shaping.

Back

- Using size E/4 crochet hook, size 3 needle, and crochet-chain cast on (see page 126), CO 112 (138, 164) sts. Knit 1 row, purl 1 row.
- **Pattern stitch for back:**
  Note: To keep track of where you are in lace patt, place markers between each of 13-st reps.
  Row 1: K3, *K3, YO, SSK, K5, K2tog, YO, K1*, rep from * to * to last 5 sts, K5.
  Rows 2, 4, and 6: Purl.
  Row 3: K3, *K4, YO, SSK, K3, K2tog, YO, K2*, rep from * to * to last 5 sts, K5.
  Row 5: K3, *K2, YO, SSK, K1, YO, SSK, K1, K2tog, YO, K1, K2tog, YO*, rep from * to * to last 5 sts, K5.
  Work above 6-row rep a total of 17 (19, 21) times, inc 1 st at each side on rows 20, 40, 60, 80, and 100, work additional sts as St st—122 (148, 174) sts.
- **Shape armholes:** BO 8 (12, 16) sts at beg of next 2 rows, dec 1 st at each side every RS row 8 (12, 16) times—90 (100, 110) sts.

Note: Keep at least 5 sts at armhole edge in St st.

- Work even in patt until piece measures 7¼ (8, 8¾)", ending with a completed WS row.
- **Shape back neck:** Keeping at least 5 sts at either side of back neck shaping in St st, work 31 (35, 39) sts, BO middle 28 (30, 32) sts, work rem 31 (35, 39) sts. Work each side separately.
- **Left side:** Dec 1 st on each RS row at neck edge 3 times, AT SAME TIME at beg of next 3 WS rows, BO as foll: 9 (10, 12) sts, 9 (11, 12) sts, and 10 (11, 12) sts.
- **Right side:** Work as for left side, but BO shoulders on RS rows.

Border

Stitches are picked up around the perimeter of the sweater and worked in garter stitch, then mitering is done at the two front bottoms and two front tops.

- Sew shoulder and side seams.
- With RS facing, size 1 circ needle, and beg at left side seam, PU 110 (136, 162) sts along back bottom; 56 (69, 82) sts along right front bottom, marking off last st as corner st; 121 (135, 151) sts up right front, marking off last st here for corner st; 103 (115, 127) sts around neck, marking off last st here for corner st; 121 (135, 151) sts down left front, marking off last st here for corner st; and 56 (69, 82) sts along lower left front. Place a different colored marker for beg and end of rnd—567 (659, 755) sts.
  Row 1: Purl, inc 1 st before and after each marked-off corner st. Inc by doing a firm backward loop over needle (see page 128).
  Row 2: Knit.
  Rep these 2 rows 4 times for a total of 4 ridges.
- **Picot bind off:** Sl last st worked to size 1 steel crochet hook, *ch 4, put next 2 sts from needle on hook, YO and pull through all 3

sts on hook*, rep from * to * until all sts are used up. To finish, ch 4, sl st into base of first picot.

SLEEVES

- Using size E/4 crochet hook, size 3 needle, and crochet-chain cast on, CO 54 (67, 80) sts. Knit 1 row, purl 1 row.
- **Pattern stitch for sleeves:**
  Row 1: *K3, YO, SSK, K5, K2tog, YO, K1*, rep from * to * to last 2 sts, K2.
  Rows 2, 4, and 6: Purl.
  Row 3: *K4, YO, SSK, K3, K2tog, YO, K2*, rep from * to * to last 2 sts, K2.
  Row 5: *K2, YO, SSK, K1, YO, SSK, K1, K2tog, YO, K1, K2tog, YO*, rep from * to * to last 2 sts, K2.
  Work in above lace patt, inc 1 st at each side every 6 rows 7 times—68 (81, 94) sts—then every 12 rows 8 times—84 (97, 110) sts. Work all inc in St st, keeping middle 54 (67, 80) sts in lace patt as established.

- Work even until piece measures 16¼ (16½, 17)", ending with a completed WS row.
- **Shape cap:** Working at least 5 sts on either side of all decs in St st, BO 8 (12, 16) sts at beg of next 2 rows—68 (73, 78) sts. Dec 1 st at each side every RS row 8 (12, 16) times—52 (49, 46) sts. Dec 1 st at each side every other RS row 6 times—40 (37, 34) sts. Work 1 WS row. BO 2 sts at beg of next 6 rows, working last row before final BO in St st. BO rem 28 (25, 22) sts.
- **Sleeve border:** With size 1 needle and RS facing, PU 52 (65, 78) sts around bottom of sleeve. Knit 7 rows; work picot bind off as for back.

FINISHING

- Sew sleeves into armholes; sew sleeve and side seams.
- Sew button to top of left band. Slip the button into one of the picot loops on the right band to fasten.

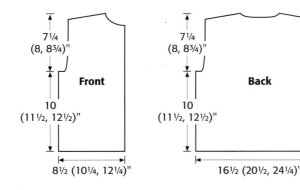

Front
7¼ (8, 8¾)"
10 (11½, 12½)"
8½ (10¼, 12¼)"

Back
7¼ (8, 8¾)"
10 (11½, 12½)"
16½ (20½, 24¼)"

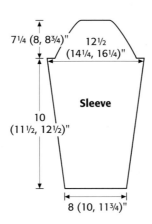

Sleeve
7¼ (8, 8¾)" 12½ (14¼, 16¼)"
10 (11½, 12½)"
8 (10, 11¾)"

Beaded Pulse Warmers

PATTERNED AND BEADED pulse warmers were in fashion all over Norway until around 1920; today they remain a part of the Norwegian national costume. They were originally used for practical purposes: to cover up frayed or dirty cuffs or to disguise too-short sleeves on children who were outgrowing their clothing. My friend Arnhild Hillesland first introduced them to me when I was at her weekend knitting retreat in Iowa. I fell in love with them, since I love both beads and yarn. I have tried to make the beaded pattern of these somewhat echo the lovely lace pattern of Cornflower Cardigan.

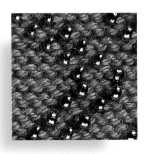

MATERIALS

- 1 skein Richesse et Soie from K1C2 Gourmet Collection (65% cashmere, 35% silk; 25 grams, 145 yards per skein), color Cornflower Blue*, or other sport-weight yarn
- Small amount of waste yarn for provisional CO
- One set of double-pointed needles, size 1 (2.25 mm) or size needed to obtain gauge
- Size B/1 (2.25 mm) crochet hook
- 400 size 8/0 seed beads
- Bead needle

*10 grams of yarn were used, so yarn left over from Cornflower Cardigan would most likely be enough for a pair.

GAUGE

9½ sts and 19 rows = 1" in garter stitch on size 1 needles

FINISHED MEASUREMENTS

CIRCUMFERENCE: 5½"
WIDTH: 2½"

PATTERN STITCH

Garter Stitch
Knit every row.

PULSE WARMERS
(MAKE 2 EXACTLY THE SAME)

- Thread 200 beads onto yarn. (You will need only 192 for each pulse warmer, but it's insurance to have a few extra.)
- Provisionally CO 24 sts (see page 126).
  Foundation row (RS): Knit 1 row. From now on, always sl first st of every row pw wyif.
  Row 1 (WS): Knit row 1 from chart, placing beads on RS of work.
  Row 2 and all other RS rows not shown on chart: Knit.
  Cont in above manner, working 1 row of knit on RS and foll chart for WS rows.
- Rep 33 rows of chart 3 times, remembering to work a RS row after each row 33.
- Carefully pull out provisional CO and place live sts on needle. Holding both needles tog WS to WS, work three-needle bind off (see page 126).

Pulse Warmer

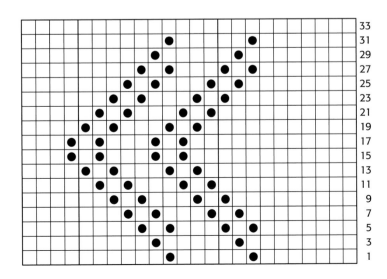

5½"
(before bind off)

2½"

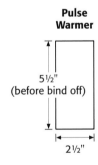

● Place bead.

Silk

Machinery in Hanks Hill Silk Mill (Photo by David Wagner)

*I*N FRONT OF the Old Town Hall in Mansfield Center, Connecticut, stands a lone mulberry tree. The University of Connecticut, the town's main industry, is just a few miles down the road. Two hundred years ago, the villages of Mansfield were host to a different industry, that of sericulture, or silk production. This mulberry tree is one of the few reminders that Mansfield had the first operating silk mill in the country.

The ancient Chinese discovered that the cocoons of wild silkworms could be unwound, and the filaments woven into luxurious and smooth fabrics. A little later came the discovery that these wild worms could be cultivated; the quality and color of the resulting filament could be controlled by what they were fed. The worms were pampered and fussed over, and the miraculous fiber they produced was so highly prized that it was reserved for royalty alone. Chinese myths date sericulture to 2,640 B.C., and it was kept such a closely guarded secret that silk production was not known in Europe until almost 3,200 years later. The worldwide industry of silk production was begun in 552 A.D. by two monks who smuggled silkworm eggs from China to Europe.

Consider some of the properties of this incredible fiber. Spun as a semi-liquid, which hardens when it comes in contact with the air, the surface of a silk fiber is extremely smooth and shiny. Being warm and lightweight, silk has the same insulating qualities as cashmere and is used when warmth without bulk is desired, as in undergarments. It has amazing hygroscopicity, or the ability to absorb moisture without feeling wet, absorbing 30% of its dry weight in moisture and still not feeling wet to the touch. Add its elastic capability to all the above, being able to stretch 10% to 20% over its length without breaking, and you have one super fiber! All of this can be attributed to one little amazing insect, the *Bombyx mori*.

Its life is short but intense. About ¼" in length when hatched, the worm is raised through four moltings and increases to about 3½" in length. It starts spinning its cocoon about 30 days after hatching and goes into the pupa state for 15 to 17 days.

Silkworm (Photo by David Wagner)

Cocoons measure about 1½" long and ¾" wide.

After breaking out of the cocoon, it mates immediately, and in the course of three days, the average female will lay more than 350 eggs.

Cultivated silkworms eat only mulberry leaves. Approximately 2,660 pounds of mulberry leaves are required for every ounce of worms. One ounce of worms produces roughly 150 to 160 ounces of silk. It is estimated that one acre of trees is required to produce one pound of silk.

Silkworms on Mulberry Leaves (Photo by Kenneth Strick)

Wild silk, called tussah, is usually colored, depending on what the worms eat. They may eat anything from plum leaves to oak leaves, and depending on the tannin present in what they eat, their silk is usually not white. The fiber is coarser and is typically used in carpets.

To make one pound of raw silk, 2,500 to 3,000 cocoons are needed, each cocoon yielding

about 600 yards. When sericulture was a cottage industry, cocoons were reeled by hand. They first had to be soaked in water to soften the gum coating on the threads. The tiny end of the filament was found by carefully brushing the outside of the cocoon, and then the tedious process of hand reeling the filaments would begin. An average yield of hand reeling would be about 1 to 2 pounds of silk per week. Usually six or seven cocoons would be reeled together, but if each cocoon were reeled separately, it would require 1,800,000 yards, or 1000 miles of a single filament to weigh 1 pound!

Before the fiber can be dyed, it first has to go through an ungumming process. It is boiled in soap and water, which reduces its weight by an astounding 25%. With the advent of industrial refinement for the reeling process occurring in the 14th century, silk became the first fiber to be produced industrially.

The first effort of sericulture in America began as early as 1632, when James I halted the cultivation of tobacco in Virginia in order to begin the raising of mulberry trees. I live on Wormwood Hill Road; the crossroad that is just down the street is Mulberry Road. Just a short way through the woods is the site of the first silk mill in America. In 1810 Rodney and Horace Hanks built a mill to produce silk and silk twist. It was in operation for about 10 years, but failed because the machinery was not sophisticated enough to handle the incredibly delicate filaments.

There were several other mills scattered around the villages of Mansfield, but eventually they, too, closed down.

During the early 1800s, sericulture was viewed as easy supplemental income. Colonial housewives and children would tend to the worms, keeping them stacked in trays in their parlors. Fresh mulberry leaves were collected each day for the worms to munch on. In a short time they would spin their cocoons. Once the cocoon was spun, the pupa inside had to be killed. If it broke out of the cocoon, the delicate threads would be broken and it would be impossible to reel one continuous strand of filament. The death sentence was carried out by either boiling the cocoon, or weather permitting, baking them outside in the hot sun. Ten pounds of cocoons could be sold for about $50.

While this process may have brought a little extra money into the household, the negative side effects that sericulture produced most likely led to its demise. Because the worms can only feed on mulberry leaves, the demand drove the price of the trees so high that the trees themselves became more valuable than their end product of silk. But the ultimate demise of Colonial America's silk industry was Mother Nature. In 1844, a mulberry blight spread, killing off almost all of the trees. Most of the small mills in New England were ruined, but a few were able to continue production by using raw silk imported from China.

Few people in this country raise silkworms anymore, but Ann Galonska, president of the Mansfield Historical Society, still does. She became intrigued by the silk history of Mansfield and decided to give it a try. After a few failures, she finally succeeded in raising the worms and harvesting the cocoons. She shares her fascination about these delicate creatures with the town's school children. She travels with her worms and silk paraphernalia to the elementary schools, where the children listen to her tell about the life cycle of the worm, view the worms up close munching on their mulberry leaves, and try hand reeling the filaments from a cocoon.

Knitting and Designing with Silk

Two of the projects in this book use 100% silk: Caroline's Sweater (page 60) and Magic Colors Silk Stole (page 68). Several other projects use a blend of silk with other fibers. These yarns do not pose any problem. The content of other fibers is sufficient to offset the difficulty that sometimes arises when working with 100% silk.

Silk has no memory. This means that if stretched, it does not go back to its original shape. This ability is what makes silk such a strong fiber, but alas, poses problems for hand knitters. This knowledge was tucked into my brain as I began designing and calculating numbers for the silk stole. My initial concept was that the stole was to be 80" by 22". After swatching on size 9 needles and doing my calculations, I knit the stole and tried it on. It stretched down to the floor and pooled around my ankles! The truth about silk stretching finally came into the front part of my brain. And so I ripped. After consulting with a few people, I decided to bring it down several needle sizes, reduce the number of stitches, and work the lace in garter stitch instead of stockinette. This idea worked out very well size-wise, but I didn't like the look of the garter stitch. I ripped it out yet again. Then I cast on the same number of stitches on the same-size needle, but went back to working the pattern in stockinette stitch. This was the solution. The size worked out nicely, the smoothness of the stockinette stitch showed off the silk's luster, and the smaller-size needle made a firmer fabric with less tendency to stretch.

The stitch pattern for the Magic Colors Silk Stole is beautifully balanced between lacy openness and smooth stockinette stitch.

Caroline's Sweater posed no difficulties whatsoever. The silk chenille was such a deep and rich color that the most perfect way to show it off was to use stockinette stitch. Because chenille has a rougher texture than the other two silks, stretching and sagging was not a problem. I wanted only the slightest bit of ornament to an otherwise plain sweater, so I chose the little scallops to use as a border.

A simple crocheted scallop border is all that is needed for Caroline's sumptuous sweater.

Lorna's Laces hand-dyed 50% silk/50% wool was a yarn I knew I could use for almost any garment. The wool content would give it all the stability it needed while the silk content just made it that much more beautiful. The original concept for the Star Stitch Twin Set (page 63) was for a lace surplice sweater, with the underside being knit from a darker color. The theory was that this darker color would peep through the lace holes and make an unusual and dramatic statement. I chose a pattern called Butterfly. I knit the sweater once but scrapped it because I had miscalculated the placements of the butterflies. I reknit it again,

tried it on, and hated it! It was such a beautiful concept in my head and such a terrible-looking real item. Not only did the darker color not show through the lace holes at all, but the entire thing fit and hung poorly. The fault lay not with the yarn, but with my calculations. And so I ripped—again.

This time I re-skeined and washed all the yarn to get the kinks out. For my third attempt, I changed direction, this time deciding on a twin set, with a lace-stitch cardigan knit from the lighter color, and a shell knit from the darker color. I was still adamant about this dramatic dark color showing through a lace pattern. But this time I made sure the lace pattern had more holes, and I changed my calculations for fit.

The solid dark color of the Star Stitch shell adds a nice contrast to the light-colored lace pattern of the Star Stitch cardigan.

A simple crochet edging was all that was required to finish off the cardigan. In contrast to this very pretty, feminine sweater, the shell is a smooth and plain stockinette stitch.

Caroline's Sweater

THIS YARN IS SO luxurious and the color so beautiful that to use anything other than the plainest stitch is unnecessary. Adding the little scallops for the border was the only ornamentation I thought it required. I named this sweater after the very talented and lovely person who dyed the yarn, Caroline McInnis. Wear the silk against your skin for maximum tactile effect!

MATERIALS

- 5 (6, 7, 8) skeins 100% Silk Chenille from Sweaterkits.com (100% silk; 56 grams, 186 yards per skein), color Deep Blue, or other sport-weight yarn
- Size 3 (3.25 mm) needles or size needed to obtain gauge
- Size 3 (3.25 mm) circular needle (16")
- Size 4 (3.5 mm) needles
- Size E/4 (3.50 mm) crochet hook
- Stitch holders
- Stitch marker

FINISHED MEASUREMENTS

BUST: 38 (42, 46, 50)"
CENTER BACK LENGTH: 19¼ (21, 22¾, 24½)"

GAUGE

24½ sts and 34 rows = 4" in stockinette stitch on size 3 needles

PATTERN STITCHES

Stockinette Stitch (for body)
Knit all RS rows; purl all WS rows.

Scalloped Border
Multiple of 11 plus 2

Row 1 (WS): Purl.
Row 2: K2, *K1, sl this st back to LH needle, lift the next 8 sts, one at a time, from LH needle over this st and off the needle, YO twice, knit the first st again, K2*, rep from * to * to end.
Row 3: K1, *P2tog, knit into the front and back of each of the loops made from YO in previous row (4 sts made from 2 loops), P1 * rep from * to * to last st, K1.
Rows 4–7: Knit.

BACK

- With size 4 needles and long-tail cast on (see page 125), CO 211 (233, 255, 277) sts.
- Work 7 rows of scalloped border—19 (21, 23, 25) scallops and 116 (128, 140, 152) sts.
- Change to size 3 needles and work in St st for 12 (13, 14, 15)".
- **Shape raglan:** BO 10 (12, 14, 16) sts at beg of next 2 rows—96 (104, 112, 120) sts. Work raglan dec patt (rows 1–6) as foll a total of 12 times, then rep rows 1–3 once more.
  Rows 1 and 2: Work in St st.
  Row 3 (RS, raglan dec): K3, sl 1, K1, psso, knit to last 5 sts, K2tog, K3.
  Rows 4 and 5: Work in St st.
  Row 6 (WS, raglan dec): P3, P2tog, purl to last 5 sts, P2tog tbl, P3.
- **Rows 7–76 (85, 91, 100):** Work even—46 (48, 52, 54) sts.
- **Shape back neck:**
  Row 77 (86, 92, 101): Work 6 sts, work middle 34 (36, 40, 42) sts and place on holder for back neck, work rem 6 sts. Work each side separately, remembering to work appropriately slanting decreases on rows 3 and 6 as above.
  Row 78 (87, 93, 102): Work raglan dec at armhole edge—5 sts.
  Row 79 (88, 94, 103): Dec 1 st at neck edge—4 sts.
  Row 80 (89, 95, 104): Work even.
  Row 81 (90, 96, 105): Dec 1 st at neck edge—3 sts.
  Row 82 (91, 97, 106): Work even.
  Row 83 (92, 98, 107): K1, K2tog, pass second st over first st.
- Break yarn and draw through loop to fasten off.

FRONT

- Work as for back, working raglan dec 20 (21, 22, 24) times. Work 1 row even—56 (62, 68, 72) sts and 61 (64, 67, 73) rows.
- **Shape front neck:** Work 16 (20, 22, 24) sts, work middle 24 (22, 24, 24) sts and place on holder for front neck, work rem 16 (20, 22, 24) sts. Work each side separately.
- Beg on next row, work raglan dec patt (rows 1–6) at armhole edge a total of 2 (3, 4, 4) times, then rows 1–3 another 1 (1, 0, 1) time, and AT SAME TIME dec 1 st at neck edge every 3 rows 5 (7, 8, 9) times—6 sts.
- Work 2 rows even.
- Work rows 78 (87, 93, 102) through rows 83 (92, 98, 107) as for back.

SLEEVES

- With size 4 needles, CO 90 (101, 112, 123) sts.
- Work 7 rows of scalloped border as for back—50 (56, 62, 68) sts. Change to size 3 needles and work rem of sleeve in St st.
- Inc 1 st at each side every 10 (7, 7, 6) rows 5 (7, 8, 10) times, then every 8 rows 12 times—84 (94, 102, 112) sts.
- Work 2 rows even.

- **Shape cap:** BO 10 (12, 14, 16) sts at beg of next 2 rows—64 (70, 74, 80) sts. Dec 1 st at each side every 3 rows 27 (30, 32, 35) times, working dec same as for back. Work 1 (0, 0, 1) row even. BO rem 10 sts.

FINISHING

- Sew raglan sleeve seams to front and back body. Sew each sleeve seam.
- **Neck:** With RS facing, size 3 circ needle, and starting at middle of right sleeve top, PU 9 sts down right back, K34 (36, 40, 42) sts from back neck holder, PU 9 sts up left back, PU 15 sts down left front, K24 (22, 24, 24) sts from front neck holder, PU 15 sts up right front, pm—106 (106, 112, 114) sts. (Purl 1 rnd, knit 1 rnd) 2 times. BO very loosely in knit, but do not break yarn and do not pull thread through last st. Instead, put this last st on crochet hook.
- Work scalloped crochet (see page 131) border for neck as foll: *Sc in each of next 2 sts, 8 dc into next st*, rep from * to * to end. Sl last st through sc to fasten off.
- You may hand wash the sweater and lay it flat to dry, or dry-clean.

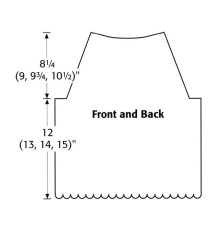

8¼ (9, 9¾, 10½)"

Front and Back

12 (13, 14, 15)"

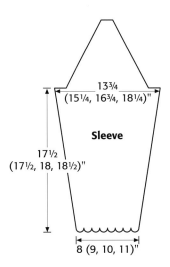

13¾ (15¼, 16¾, 18¼)"

Sleeve

17½ (17½, 18, 18½)"

8 (9, 10, 11)"

Star Stitch Twin Set

KNIT THIS ELEGANT little twin set in two of Lorna's beautiful dyed-to-match colors. The darker color of the shell will show ever so subtly through the lacy holes of the Star Stitch cardigan. Three-quarter-length sleeves make it comfortable and sophisticated for evening wear.

Cardigan

MATERIALS

- 3 skeins Helen's Lace from Lorna's Laces (50% silk, 50% wool; 113 grams, 1250 yards per skein), color Powder Blue (use double strand throughout), or other lace-weight yarn used doubled
- Size 4 (3.5 mm) needle or size needed to obtain gauge
- Size E/4 (3.5 mm) crochet hook
- 1 small button

GAUGE

23½ sts and 34 rows = 4" in pattern stitch on size 4 needles

FINISHED MEASUREMENTS

BUST: 39 (43, 46, 49)"
TOTAL BACK LENGTH: 19½ (20½, 22, 23½)"

PATTERN STITCH

Multiple of 3
Foundation row: Knit.
Row 1 (WS): Purl.
Row 2: K2, *YO, K3, pass first of 3 knit sts over second and third st*, rep from * to * to last st, K1.
Row 3: Purl.
Row 4: K1, *K3, pass first of 3 knit sts over second and third st, YO*, rep from * to * to last 2 sts, K2.
Rep these 4 rows for patt.

BACK

- With 2 strands of yarn held tog, CO 114 (126, 135, 144) sts. Work in patt until piece measures 12 (13, 14, 15)", ending with a completed WS row.
  NOTE: Do not work patt on RS rows any closer than 3 sts from side edge.
- **Shape armholes:** BO 8 sts at beg of next 2 rows—98 (110, 119, 128) sts. Work RS row.
- Beg on next row, dec 1 st at each side edge every WS row 7 (7, 10, 10) times—84 (96, 99, 108) sts.
- Work even until armholes measure 7½ (7½, 8, 8½)", ending with a completed RS row.
- **Shape shoulders and back neck (WS):** Work 30 (35, 37, 39) sts, BO middle 24 (26, 25, 30) sts, work rem 30 (35, 37, 39) sts. Work each side separately.
- **Right side:** At beg of next 2 RS rows BO 9 (10, 11, 12) sts and 9 (11, 11, 12) sts, AT SAME TIME dec 1 st at neck edge on next 2 WS rows. BO 9 (11, 12, 12) sts, dec 1 st at neck edge.
- **Left side:** Attach yarn at neck edge on RS and work as for left side, reversing all shaping.

RIGHT FRONT

- With 2 strands of yarn held tog CO 58 (64, 67, 73) sts. Work foundation row.
  Row 1: K1, work patt row 1.
  Row 2: P1, work patt row 2.
  Row 3: K1, work patt row 3.
  Row 4: P1, work patt row 4.
  Keeping 1 st at center front edge as established, work in patt until piece measures same length as back to armhole.
- **Shape armhole (WS):** BO 8 sts—50 (56, 59, 65) sts. Dec 1 st at armhole edge every WS row 7 (7, 10, 10) times—43 (49, 49, 55) sts.
- Work even in patt until piece measures 3½".

- **Shape neck:** Keeping 1 st at center edge as established, dec 1 st every RS row 16 (17, 15, 19) times—27 (32, 34, 36) sts. (Decs are worked as foll: knit center front edge st, SSK, work to end of row.)
- Work even until piece measures same as back to beg of shoulder shaping, ending with a completed RS row.
- At beg of next 3 WS rows BO as foll: 9 (10, 11, 12) sts, 9 (11, 11, 12) sts, and 9 (11, 12, 12) sts.

LEFT FRONT

Work as for right front, reversing all shaping and working center front dec as foll: work to last 3 sts, K2tog, knit center front edge st.

SLEEVES

- CO 75 (78, 81, 84) sts. Work even in patt until piece measures 3½".
- Beg on next row, inc 1 st at each side every 1½" 3 times, then every 1" 4 times, and then every ½" 2 times—93 (96, 99, 102) sts.
- Work even until piece measures 12 (12½, 13, 13½)", ending with a completed WS row.
  Note: Do not work patt on RS rows any closer than 3 sts from side edge.
- **Shape cap:** BO 8 sts at beg of next 2 rows—77 (80, 83, 86) sts. Work RS row. Beg on next row, dec 1 st at each side every WS row 7 (7, 10, 10) times—63 (66, 63, 66) sts.
- Work even until sleeve cap measures 3¾ (3½, 4¼, 5½)", ending with a completed RS row. Dec 1 st at each side every other WS row 6 (7, 6, 7) times—51 (52, 51, 52) sts. BO 2 sts at beg of next 6 rows—39 (40, 39, 40) sts. BO rem sts as foll: *K2tog 2 times, pass first st over second st *, rep from * to * to last 3 (0, 3, 0) sts, K3tog, pass first st over second st. Fasten off.

FINISHING

- Sew shoulder seams and body side seams. Sew sleeve seams and sew sleeves into armholes.
- **Body edging:** With RS facing and starting at lower right side seam, sc around entire perimeter of sweater, making sure edges lie flat. Work 3 sc into lower right corner, upper right neck corner at beg of neck dec, upper left neck corner at end of neck dec, and lower left corner. Join with sl st into first sc. Work foll rnd around entire sweater: *Ch 3, sk 1 st, 2 sc in next st*, rep from * to * to end. Join with a sl st into first ch 3. Fasten off.
- **Sleeve edging:** Work as for body edging.
- Do not press, but rather steam very lightly by hovering iron over piece.
- **Fastening:** Fasten with one small button, using the ch-3 space on opposite side as a buttonhole.

Shell

MATERIALS

- 2 skeins Helen's Lace from Lorna's Laces, color Pond Blue (Use double strand throughout.)
- Small amount of waste yarn for provisional CO
- Size 1 (2.25 mm) circular needle (29")
- Size 2 (2.75 mm) circular needle (16")
- Size 4 (3.5 mm) circular needle (29") or size needed to obtain gauge
- Stitch markers
- Stitch holders

GAUGE

26 sts and 36 rows = 4" in pattern on size 4 needles

Finished Measurements

Bust: 35 (38, 40½, 43½)"
Total Back Length: 19½ (20½, 22, 23)"

Pattern Stitch

Stockinette Stitch
In the rnd: Knit every rnd.
Back and forth: Knit row 1 (RS) and purl row 2.

Body

- With size 1 needle, crochet hook, and 2 strands of yarn held tog, provisionally CO 228 (246, 264, 282) sts (see page 126), join, pm. Work in patt for 1", purl 1 rnd. Change to size 4 needle and work in patt for 1".
- **Attach hem:** Carefully pull out provisional CO and place these sts on size 1 needle. Fold hem up and place size 1 needle behind size 4 needle. Knit 1 st from front needle and 1 st from back needle tog; rep across. Place second marker after 114 (123, 132, 141) sts.
- Work in patt, dec 1 st at each side of each marker every 1½" 3 times—216 (234, 252, 270) sts. Work dec as foll: K2tog at beg of rnd, knit to 2 sts before second marker, SSK, sl marker, K2tog, knit to 2 sts before first marker, SSK.
- Inc 1 st at each side of each marker every 1½" 3 times—228 (246, 264, 282) sts. Work inc as foll: K1, M1 right, knit to 1 st before second marker, M1 left, K1, sl marker, K1, M1 right, knit to 1 st before first marker, M1 left, K1.
- Work until entire piece measures 12 (13, 14, 15)".

- **Front:** Work on half of sts for front; put other sts on holder for back. BO 4 (5, 6, 7) sts at beg of next 2 rows, then BO 2 sts at beg of next 4 rows—98 (105, 112, 119) sts. Dec 1 st at each edge on each RS row 7 (8, 9, 10) times—84 (89, 94, 99) sts.
- Work even until armhole measures 6 (6, 6½, 7)", ending with a completed WS row.
- **Shape front neck:** Work 35 (37, 39, 41) sts, place middle 14 (15, 16, 17) sts on holder for front neck. Work each side separately.
- **Left side:** At beg of next 3 RS rows, BO as foll: 3 sts, 3 sts, and 2 sts. Dec 1 st at neck edge at beg of next 5 (6, 6, 7) WS rows—22 (23, 25, 26) sts.
- **Shape shoulders:** At beg of next 3 RS rows BO as foll: 7 (7, 8, 8) sts, 7 (8, 8, 9) sts, and 8 (8, 9, 9) sts. (Or work short rows; see pages 129–30.)
- **Right side:** Attach yarn at neck edge and work as for left side, reversing all shaping.
- **Back:** Work as for front, omitting neck shaping, until exact same length to beg of shoulder shaping, ending with a completed WS row. Work 22 (23, 25, 26) sts, place middle 40 (43, 44, 47) sts on holder for back neck. Work each side separately.
- Shape shoulders as for front.

FINISHING

- Sew shoulder seams.
- **Neckband:** With RS facing, size 2 needle, and beg at right shoulder seam, PU 5 sts down right back, K 40 (43, 44, 47) sts from back neck holder, PU 5 sts up left back, PU 20 sts down left front, K 14 (15, 16, 17) sts from front neck holder, PU 20 sts up right front, pm—104 (108, 110, 114) sts. Knit 4 rnds, purl 1 rnd, knit 4 rnds, dec 10 (10, 11, 11) sts on second rnd. Turn hem at purl rnd and use live sts to sew hem down (see page 129).
- **Armholes:** With RS facing, size 2 needle, and starting at underarm, PU 39 (41, 43, 45) sts to shoulder, PU another 39 (41, 43, 45) sts to underarm—78 (82, 86, 90) sts. Work as for neckband.

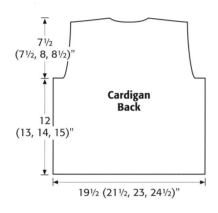

7½
(7½, 8, 8½)"

12
(13, 14, 15)"

Cardigan Back

19½ (21½, 23, 24½)"

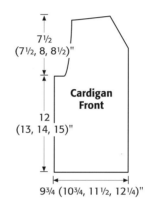

7½
(7½, 8, 8½)"

12
(13, 14, 15)"

Cardigan Front

9¾ (10¾, 11½, 12¼)"

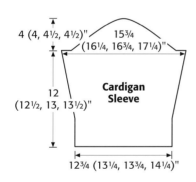

4 (4, 4½, 4½)"

15¾
(16¼, 16¾, 17¼)"

12
(12½, 13, 13½)"

Cardigan Sleeve

12¾ (13¼, 13¾, 14¼)"

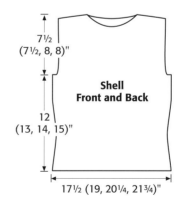

7½
(7½, 8, 8)"

12
(13, 14, 15)"

Shell Front and Back

17½ (19, 20¼, 21¾)"

Magic Colors Silk Stole

MY FRIEND Charlene Schurch, besides being an incredible knitwear designer and author, is a dye genius. She has taken nine colors of one-ply silk, organized them in specific lengths, and then put them together to make a Magic Ball of three-ply yarn. The colors go imperceptibly from green to gold. The stole is knit in the simplest of patterns, but as you knit, watch the magic that unfolds from this wonderful ball of yarn!

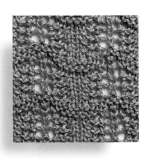

MATERIALS

- 1 Magic Ball of 100% Silk 3 ply (336 grams, 1260 yards), color green to gold, or other DK-weight yarn
- Size 4 (3.5 mm) circular needle (29") or size needed to obtain gauge
- Size E/4 (3.5 mm) crochet hook

GAUGE

18 sts and 36 rows = 4" in pattern stitch on size 4 needles

FINISHED MEASUREMENTS

Approximately 50 (60)" long x 21" wide

PATTERN STITCH

Multiple of 12 plus 1
Rows 1–4: Knit.
Row 5 (RS): K1, *K2tog 2 times, (YO, K1) 3 times, YO, (sl 1 kw, K1, psso) 2 times, K1*, rep from * to *.
Row 6: Purl.
Rows 7–12: Rep rows 5 and 6 another 3 times.

Here is another example of the color changes in Charlene's truly magical yarn.

STOLE

- Using crochet-chain cast on (see page 126), CO 259 (307) sts. Work as follows:
  Row 1: K3, work row 1 of patt over middle 253 (301) sts, K3.
  Row 2: Sl first st pw wyif, K2, work row 2 of patt over middle 253 (307) sts, K3.
  Rows 3–12: Cont in above manner, always working 3 border sts at beg and end of row as for row 2 and working appropriate patt row over middle 253 (301) sts. Work 12-row patt rep 15 times. BO in knit.
- **Ruffled edging:** With RS facing, PU 1 st in each bound-off st—259 (307) sts.
  Row 1: Purl.
  Row 2: Knit into front and back of each st—518 (614) sts.
  Row 3: Purl.
  Rows 4 and 5: Rep rows 2 and 3—1036 (1228) sts.
- BO in knit.

FINISHING

- The Magic Ball will have knots in only 1 of the 3 plies. These are very small and can be made to stay on the wrong side of the work. You may knit in the ends as you go along, or weave them in when you are finished.
- Do not press with hot iron, but rather hover iron over stole and press steam button to eject steam. You may stretch lace as much or as little as you wish in this manner.

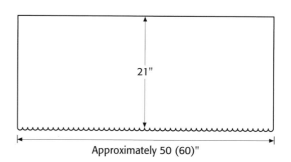

21"

Approximately 50 (60)"

Angora

Benjamin Bunny (Photo by Kenneth Strick)

I AM TEMPTED to say my favorite fiber is angora. Not necessarily because I love the fiber more than any other luxury fiber, but for the love of my English Angora rabbit named Benjamin Bunny. The small amounts of incredibly soft and beautiful fiber he gives is the added bonus of having the privilege of knowing him.

While at a fiber fair, fate decided that I should take home an Angora bunny. He was fawn colored, too cute to describe, and his fur was ethereal fluff. The ensuing weeks taught me a lot about owning a house bunny. They are neat and tidy, cage training themselves. The one drawback is that they like to chew—everything. It takes a bit of creative ingenuity to protect things, but I shrug and call it a new decorating scheme.

There are no Angora rabbits that live in the wild. It is speculated that at some point, centuries ago, rabbits were selectively bred for fiber length and quality, producing the species we know today. Presumably these animals were called angora because their coats resembled the long and silky hair of the Angora goat. Sweet and gentle, they are small and easy to care for and give fiber that is cloud soft. Sadly, it is this very fiber that is often a cause of their death. Rabbits, like cats, groom themselves by licking. Cats can cough up excess fur balls; rabbits can't. If the wool becomes impacted in their digestive tract, they get "wool block," a condition that is fatal unless caught in its early stages. Certain enzymes found in pineapple and papaya actually break down the protein of the wool, letting it pass harmlessly through the digestive system. If given daily, these foods can actually prevent wool block.

In America, the 1930s and 1940s saw angora farming at its peak. Unfortunately, with the advent of synthetics right after World War II, angora production came to an abrupt halt. It was also during this time that mink became a popular rage. With no market for their wool, many rabbit breeders sold their herds as mink food (this very thought makes my heart shudder), and angora fiber became a scarcity. Nowadays, with the resurgent interest in spinning and knitting and the popularity of natural fiber, angora production is once again flourishing.

It is hard to imagine that these engaging and endearing animals can be useful for anything other than eliciting smiles from all who gaze upon them, but these little creatures are powerhouses of wool production and no one can resist petting them on the hoof or in the skein.

Angoras come in breeds that sound like nationalities—English, German, French—while other breeds sound like descriptions—Giant, Satin, and Jersey Wooley. A rabbit can weigh anywhere from 5 to 11 pounds; wool production for an average rabbit is about ½ pound per year, with the world record being over 5 pounds per year! Angoras come in a wide range of colors, from snow white to jet black, and breeders are constantly working on developing new colors. Angora takes dye very well, but care must be taken in the dyeing process so the fiber doesn't mat.

A rabbit's coat consists of four layers. The first (outer) layer of thick guard hairs act as a protective shield. Awn hair, the next layer, is slightly less coarse; and the third layer, awn fluff, becomes finer. The last layer, underwool, is a fiber of incredible fineness and softness, with a micron count of between 8 and 13. I have often observed a single hair of rabbit fur weightlessly floating through the air in my house, buoyed by unfelt air currents.

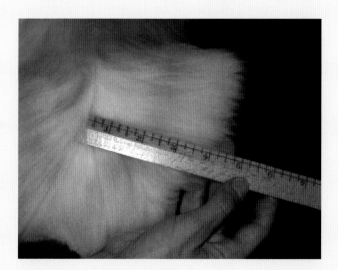

Benjamin's Fur (Photo by Kenneth Strick)

The scales of the fiber are chevron shaped, as opposed to smoother-shaped scales on other fibers. When angora is subjected to the slightest agitation, these scales become like fish hooks, grabbing onto each other and making it extremely susceptible to felting. In fact, the body heat and activity of the rabbit often matts the wool right on the body. Many times warmer than sheep's wool, it is almost impossible to wear 100% angora garments unless you live with the penguins. By blending angora with other fibers, sumptuous and luxurious skeins are born. Blending with wool, for example, gives angora the memory that it lacks while retaining the lovely ethereal haze of its fluff and making it more practical to wear in most climates.

When a rabbit's coat reaches 3" in length, it is time to harvest the wool. Like cashmere, there are two schools of thought as to how this should be accomplished. Some species—such as French, Satin, and English—will release their hair follicles so you can pluck them. I have seen spinners at fiber fairs with a rabbit on their lap, belly up, spinning the loose fibers directly from the rabbit onto their bobbins. Some claim plucking produces a better fiber, because there is no blunt end that results from clipping. Plucking is labor-intensive, and some argue that it is responsible for reduced fiber production over time because it damages the hair follicles. A plucked rabbit will also grow back a coat with a greater percentage of guard hair. Species that do not have releasing hair follicles always need to be clipped. It is faster than plucking and can be done at any time.

On a wintry day just after Christmas, my husband and I visited Ken Abert, who raises Angora rabbits in Dorchester, Massachusetts, a suburb of Boston. His 45 rabbits live in clean and spacious cages in his garage. Ken is a man possessed by his love of fiber. It begins with the rabbits themselves. Proud of every one of them, he takes certain rabbits from their cages and shows me their luxurious coats, explaining their breeds and characteristics. I admire each one in turn, then plant a kiss on their velvet noses as they are put back into their cages. Ken knows the lineage of each of his rabbits, what he would like to do to improve fiber quality and/or production, and who's ready to be clipped or plucked next. He is ever mindful of their diet and health and keeps a sharp eye on each one for any beginning signs of illness. Ken sells the rabbits and their wool at New England fiber fairs. Like most other fiber growers, he loves to use the harvest himself. The third story of his magnificent Victorian home is devoted entirely to fiber and its related paraphernalia. From looms to spinning wheels, to pickers and carders, there is everything needed to get from the rabbit to the garment. Ken dyes some of the angora and blended combinations into irresistible nests of color. They are stored in rigid plastic sandwich trays to prevent the wool from shifting and thus becoming matted. Ken asked me to choose a skein of 100% hand-spun angora from an array of beautiful skeins, and this became the muffatees I knit in honor of old Mrs. Rabbit.

As I finish up writing this chapter, I glance over to see what mischief my Benjamin has gotten into. Having had an exhausting day, he is lying on the rug, stretched out to a length of almost two feet, his powerful back legs kicked out to the side, and his little chin resting between his paws. I lean over to give his shaggy little face a caress, and so tired is he that the only recognition he can muster is a tiny flicker of one silken ear. I know he is grateful for the love and attention and will return it as soon as he catches up on his sleep.

Benjamin Bunny Napping (Photo by Kenneth Strick)

DESIGNING AND KNITTING WITH ANGORA

OF the four projects using angora, two of them use 100% hand-spun angora. Susan Emerson, of Enchanted Lace Yarns, Boulder, Colorado, spent almost a year hand spinning yarn for the Lucinda Shells Shawl (page 85). She began by blending four different dyed colors of angora, then spun and plied it into the incredible 2,275 yards, 65 wraps per inch that weighs a mere 80 grams!

From Top to Bottom: Multicolored Roving, Fluffed and Blended Colors, and the Finished Yarn for the Lucinda Shells Shawl

I played with the gossamer-thin yarn, trying to find a stitch pattern that would keep it from floating away. The knit fabric was so incredibly ethereal that it would be impossible to get into as a fitted garment. For this reason and others, I decided upon a shawl. Another yarn would most likely be substituted by knitters, and a shawl has the advantage of being finished once it reaches the desired size. After much deliberation, I decided to add a thin strand of linen to impart some body to the fabric. After washing, the angora fluffed up to a beautiful halo, and the linen softened out to add drape and body.

Ken Abert's butter-soft, naturally colored angora became muffatees (page 83) for the discriminating person who wishes to keep her hands warm in luxury. My friend Charlene shared a childhood memory with me of angora mittens knit for her by her grandmother. The mittens were so soft that she spent an entire outdoor recess with the mittens against her face so she could luxuriate in their softness.

The other two projects, White Winter Pullover (page 74) and Smocked Vest (page 80), use blends of angora. Because of their wool content, these yarns have plenty of memory and could be used in almost any garment design.

The vest, which uses Shaffhauser yarn of 70% angora, has an incredible haze of fluff over it. Because of the yarn's insulating qualities, I designed the vest in an A-line shape so it would not hug the body.

An ethereal haze makes the Smocked Vest heavenly to wear.

Kathy Haneke's sumptuous blend of white angora knit into a fabric so sinfully soft that I never wanted the White Winter Pullover project to end. A classic pullover, it can be dressed up with a black velvet skirt or worn with slacks for a more casual look. Either way, you know it's angora!

White Winter Pullover

MATERIALS

- 12 (13, 14) skeins 4/8 Sport Weight from Haneke Exotics (50% baby alpaca, 25% merino wool, 25% angora; 45 grams, 120 yards per skein), color #19 White, or other DK-weight yarn
- Size 5 (3.75 mm) straight needles
- Size 5 (3.75 mm) circular needle (16")
- Size 6 (4 mm) needles or size needed to obtain gauge
- Stitch holders
- Stitch marker

GAUGE

22 sts and 30 rows = 4" in pattern stitch on size 6 needles

FINISHED MEASUREMENTS

BUST: 38 (45½, 52½)"
CENTER BACK LENGTH: 22½ (24½, 26¾)"

PATTERN STITCH

Border
Row 1 (WS): *K1, P1*, rep from * to *.
Row 2 (RS): *YO, K2, pass YO over K2*, rep from * to *.

FRONT

Use Charts A and B.

- With size 5 straight needles, CO 102 (122, 142) sts.
- Work 2-row border patt 8 (9, 10) times—16 (18, 20) rows.
- **Next row (WS):** Purl, inc 3 sts evenly spaced—105 (125, 145) sts.
- Change to size 6 needles. For all sizes, work Chart A as foll: work first 12 sts, work 20-st rep 4 (5, 6) times, work last 13 sts.
  For sizes 38 and 52½, beg on row 1 of Chart

A and work 24 rows 4 (5) times—96 (120) rows.
For size 45½, beg on row 13 of Chart A and work through row 24, then work 24 rows of Chart A 4 times—108 rows.

- **Shape armholes:** Although Chart A does not show it, keep first 4 and last 4 sts in St st. Still foll Chart A, BO 8 (9, 10) sts at beg of next 2 rows, dec 1 st at each side every RS row 8 (10, 12) times—73 (87, 101) sts. Work dec as foll: K2, sl 1 kw, K1, psso, work to last 4 sts, K2tog, K2. When working dec, be careful to pair YO (inc) with a dec (K2tog or SKP). If there are not enough sts to do the pair, work in St st.
- After decs have been completed, work to end of Chart A, working 24 rows once again. Remember to beg and end sts where indicated.
- **Shape front neck:** Follow Chart B for your size. Work 26 (31, 36) sts, place middle 21 (25, 29) sts on holder for front neck. Work each side separately.
- **Left side:** Work WS row (row 2 of Chart B). Beg on next row, dec 1 st at neck edge every RS row 5 times—21 (26, 31) sts. Work rows 12 (12–14, 12–16) from chart B.
- **Shape shoulders:** At beg of next 3 RS rows, BO as foll: 7 (8, 10) sts, 7 (8, 10) sts, and 7 (10, 11) sts.
- **Right side:** Attach yarn to neck edge. Work rows 1 and 2 from Chart B. Shape neck and shoulders as for left side, reversing shaping.

BACK

Use Charts A and B.
- Work as for front through Chart A.
- Work first 12 (14, 16) rows of Chart B for your size, disregarding front neck shaping.
- **Shape neck and shoulders:**
  Row 13 (15, 17) (RS): BO 7 (8, 10) sts, work until there are 16 (20, 24) sts on RH

needle, place middle 27 (31, 35) sts on holder. Work each side separately.

- **Left side:**
  Row 14 (16, 18) (WS): Work in patt.
  Row 15 (17, 19) (RS): BO 7 (8, 10) sts, work in patt to 2 sts before neck edge, dec 1 st at neck edge.
  Row 16 (18, 20): Work in patt.
  Row 17 (19, 21): BO 7 (10, 11) sts, knitting last 2 sts tog before BO.
- **Right side:** Attach yarn at neck edge and work row 13 (15, 17) of chart. Work as for left side, reversing shaping.

SLEEVES

Use Chart C.

- With size 5 straight needles, CO 46 (50, 54) sts. Work border as for back.
- **Next row:** Purl, inc 1 st—47 (51, 55) sts.
- Change to size 6 needles and follow Chart C. Keep first 4 and last 4 sts in St st and remember to work YO only if there is a corresponding dec, or vice versa. Inc 1 st at each side every 6 rows 15 times, then every 3 rows 5 times—87 (91, 95) sts. Work inc as foll: P3 or K3, YO, work to last 3 sts, YO, K3 or P3.

- Work 3 (5, 5) rows even, ending with a completed WS row.
- **Cap shaping:** Decs are worked same as for back. BO 8 (9, 10) sts at beg of next 2 rows—71 (73, 75) sts. Dec 1 st at each side every RS row 10 (11, 12) times—51 sts. Work 1 row even, BO 2 sts at beg of next 14 rows. BO rem 23 sts.

FINISHING

- Sew shoulder seams.
- **Neck:** With RS facing, size 5 circ needle, and starting at right shoulder, PU 5 sts down right back, K27 (31, 35) sts from back neck holder, PU 5 sts up left back, PU 15 (17, 19) sts down left front, K21 (25, 29) sts from front neck holder, PU 15 (17, 19) sts up right front, pm—88 (100, 112) sts.
- Work 2 rows of border as for back 7 (8, 8) times. BO very loosely in knit.
- Sew sleeves into armholes; sew sleeve and side seams.
- Steam very lightly, hovering iron over garment, but *do not* press. Pressing will destroy the textured effect.

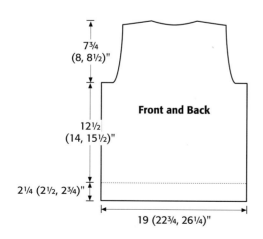

7¾ (8, 8½)"

Front and Back

12½ (14, 15½)"

2¼ (2½, 2¾)"

19 (22¾, 26¼)"

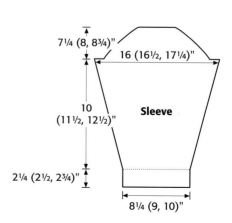

7¼ (8, 8¾)"

16 (16½, 17¼)"

10 (11½, 12½)"

Sleeve

2¼ (2½, 2¾)"

8¼ (9, 10)"

Chart A

End after
armhole
shaping is
complete.

Start after
armhole
shaping is
complete.

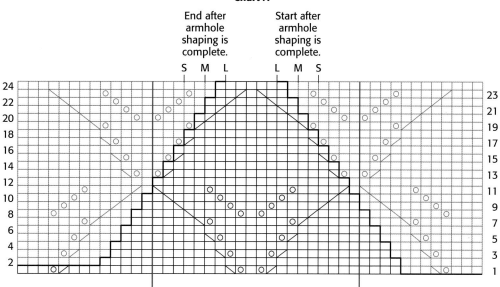

Repeat 24 rows as indicated for each size. Shape armholes following top chart.

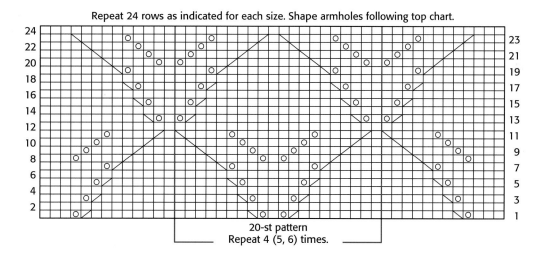

20-st pattern
Repeat 4 (5, 6) times.

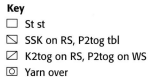

Key

☐ St st

◻ SSK on RS, P2tog tbl

◻ K2tog on RS, P2tog on WS

◻ Yarn over

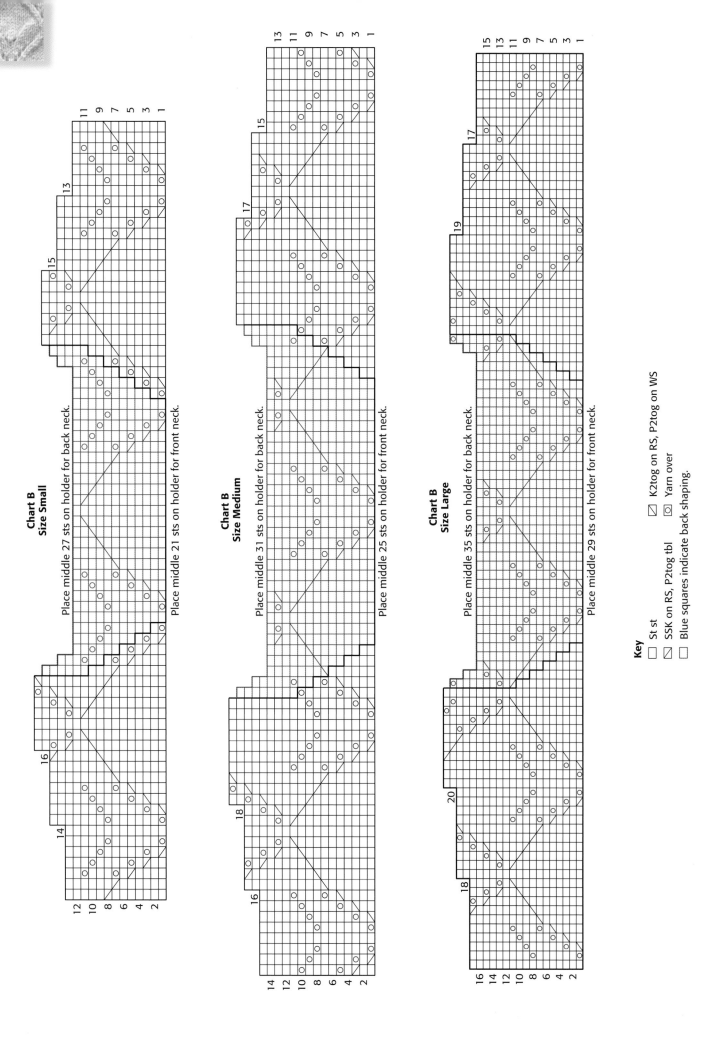

Chart B
Size Small

Place middle 27 sts on holder for back neck.

Place middle 21 sts on holder for front neck.

Chart B
Size Medium

Place middle 31 sts on holder for back neck.

Place middle 25 sts on holder for front neck.

Chart B
Size Large

Place middle 35 sts on holder for back neck.

Place middle 29 sts on holder for front neck.

Key

☐ St st
◩ SSK on RS, P2tog tbl
☐ Blue squares indicate back shaping.

◪ K2tog on RS, P2tog on WS
◯ Yarn over

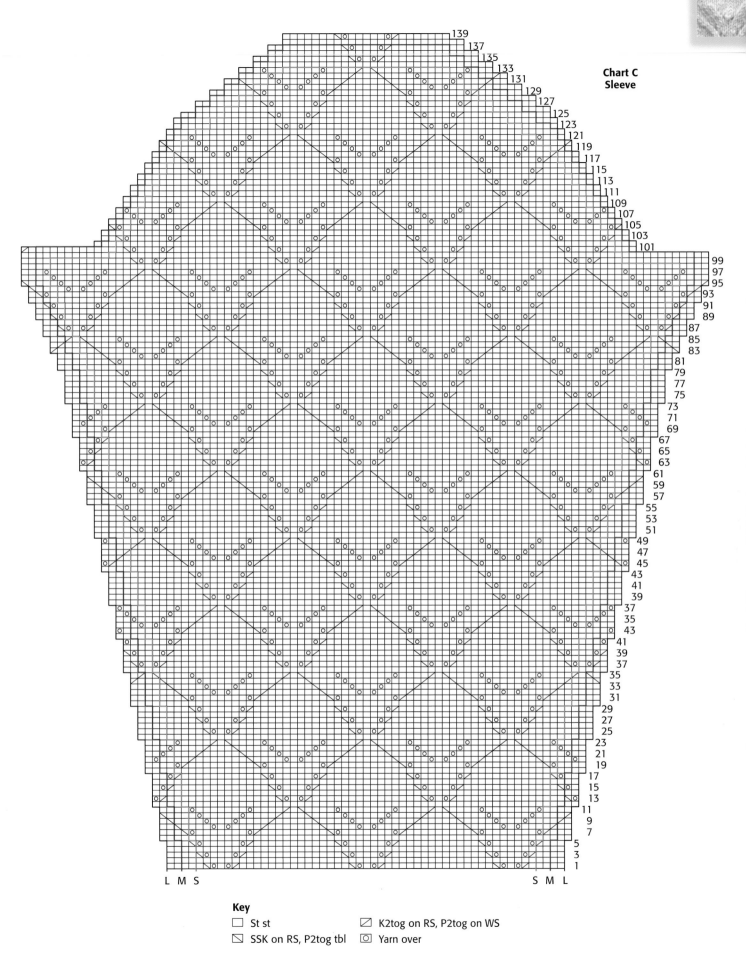

**Chart C
Sleeve**

139
137
135
133
131
129
127
125
123
121
119
117
15
13
111
109
107
105
103
101
99
97
95
93
91
89
87
85
83
81
79
77
75
73
71
69
67
65
63
61
59
57
55
53
51
49
47
45
43
41
39
37
35
43
41
39
37
35
33
31
29
27
25
23
21
19
17
15
13
11
9
7
5
3
1

L M S

S M L

Key

☐ St st

◳ K2tog on RS, P2tog on WS

◲ SSK on RS, P2tog tbl

⊡ Yarn over

Smocked Vest

This short little vest, designed to be wider at the hemline, narrows to a bare minimum across the bust. It is to be worn open, tied only at the neckline with a wisp of beads. Be careful where you wear it; people will want to pet you!

MATERIALS

- 9 (10, 11, 12, 13) skeins Schaffhauser from Skacel (70% angora, 30% virgin wool; 25 grams, 93 yards per skein), color Mustard #05, or other light worsted-weight yarn
- Size 7 (4.5 mm) straight needles or size needed to obtain gauge
- Size 7 (4.5 mm) circular needle (16")
- 4 beads

GAUGE

34½ sts and 32 rows = 4" in pattern stitch on size 7 needles

FINISHED MEASUREMENTS

Bust: 31 (35, 38½, 41½, 45½)"
BACK LENGTH: 17 (17½, 19, 20, 21½)"

PATTERN STITCH

Multiple of 8 plus 2

Row 1 and every WS row: K2, *P2, K2*, rep from * to * to end.

Row 2 (RS): P2, *K2, P2*, rep from * to * to end.

Row 4: P2, *wyib insert RH needle from front between sixth and seventh sts on LH needle and draw through a loop, sl this loop onto LH needle and knit it tog with first st, K1, P2, K2, P2*, rep from * to * to end.

Row 6: As row 2.

Row 8: P2, K2, P2, *wyib draw loop as before from between sixth and seventh sts and knit it with first st, K1, P2, K2, P2*, rep from * to * to last 4 sts, K2, P2.

Rep these 8 rows for patt.

BACK

- With straight needle, CO 146 (162, 178, 194, 210) sts. Work in patt, dec 1 st at each side every 8 rows 8 times—130 (146, 162, 178, 194) sts.
- Work even until piece measures 10 (10, 11, 12, 13)", ending with a completed WS row.
- **Shape armholes:** BO 8 sts at beg of next 2 rows, dec 1 st at each side every RS row 8 times—98 (114, 130, 146, 162) sts.
- Work even until piece measures 17 (17½, 19, 20, 21½)".
- **Shape back neck:** Work 27 (28, 30, 32, 36) sts, join a second ball of yarn and BO next 44 (58, 70, 82, 90) sts for back neck, work rem 27 (28, 30, 32, 36) sts. Working both sides at once, dec 1 st at each neck edge every RS row 2 times—25 (26, 28, 30, 34) sts for each shoulder.
- **Shape shoulders:** At beg of next 3 WS rows, BO as foll: 8 (9, 9, 10, 11) sts, 8 (9, 9, 10, 11) sts, and 9 (8, 10, 10, 12) sts.

RIGHT FRONT

- With straight needle, CO 77 (85, 93, 101, 109) sts. Work as foll:
  Row 1 (WS): Work in patt to last 3 sts, P1, sl 2 pw wyif.
  Row 2: K3, work in patt to end of row.
- Cont in patt, keeping the 3 sts at front edge as above, dec 1 st at side edge every 8 rows 8 times—69 (77, 85, 93, 101) sts.
- Work as for back, shaping armhole at side edge, until piece measures 16¼ (16½, 17¾, 18½, 19¾)"—53 (61, 69, 77, 85) sts.
- **Shape front neck:** At beg of next 3 RS rows, BO as foll: 16 (18, 21, 23, 24) sts, 3 (4, 5, 6, 7) sts, and 3 (4, 5, 6, 7) sts, then dec 1 st at neck edge every row 6 (9, 10, 12, 13) times—25 (26, 28, 30, 34) sts.
- **Shape shoulders:** Work as for back.

Left Front

- With straight needle, CO 77 (85, 93, 101, 109) sts. Work as foll:
  Row 1 (WS): P3, work in patt to end of row.
  Row 2: Work in patt to last 3 sts, K1, sl 2 pw wyib.
- Work as for right front, reversing all shaping and keeping center edge as above.

Finishing

- **Armholes:** With RS facing, circ needle, and beg at underarm, PU 100 (108, 116, 116, 124) sts around each armhole. Turn work and BO very loosely in knit from WS.

- **Neck edge:** With RS facing and circ needle, PU 28 (32, 34, 36, 38) sts to shoulder, 43 (57, 69, 81, 89) sts across back, and 28 (32, 34, 36, 38) sts from shoulder to front edge— 99 (121, 137, 153, 165) sts. Work foll 3 rows:
  Row 1 (WS): Knit.
  Row 2: *K2tog, YO*, rep from * to * to last st, K1.
  Row 3: Knit. BO very loosely.
- **Neck cord:** Cut 2 pieces of yarn each 3 yards long. Make a twisted cord (see page 131). Thread cord through eyelet openings. Sew 2 beads on ends of each cord above knot or thread beads on yarn and tie a knot.

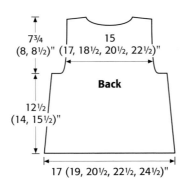

7¾ (8, 8½)" 15 (17, 18½, 20½, 22½)"

Back

12½ (14, 15½)"

17 (19, 20½, 22½, 24½)"

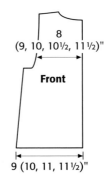

8 (9, 10, 10½, 11½)"

Front

9 (10, 11, 11½)"

Muffatees

In "The Tale of Benjamin Bunny," Beatrix Potter writes, "Old Mrs. Rabbit was a widow; she earned her living by knitting rabbit-wool mittens and muffatees (I once bought a pair at a bazaar)." Colonial housewives wore muffatees to keep their hands warm, but were still able to do their daily chores since their fingers were not covered. Their pattern was quite practical and easy; flat knitting was seamed up the side with an opening left for the thumb. I'm quite sure they knit theirs from sturdy wool and not angora! I offer you my rabbit-wool version knit in the round with a beautiful lace pattern that makes a graceful scalloped bottom.

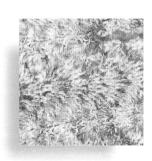

Materials for 1 Pair

- 1 skein 100% Hand Spun Angora from Dorchester Farms (56 grams, 170 yards), color Creamy White, or other sport-weight yarn
- One set of double-pointed needles, size 4 (3.5 mm) or size needed to obtain gauge
- Stitch marker

Gauge

28 sts and 32 rows = 4" in pattern stitch on size 4 needles

Finished Measurements

Circumference: 9"
Length: 7"

Pattern Stitch

Multiple of 14

In the round:
Rnds 1, 2, and 4: K1tbl, K13.
Rnd 3: K1tbl, K4tog, (YO, K1) 5 times, YO, K4tog tbl.

Back and forth:
Row 1 (RS): K1tbl, K13.
Rows 2 and 4 (WS): P13, P1tbl.
Row 3 (RS): K1tbl, K4tog, (YO, K1) 5 times, YO, K4tog tbl.

Muffatees
(make 2 exactly the same)

- CO 56 sts and join rnd, pm. Distribute sts evenly among 3 or 4 needles. Purl 3 rnds.
- Work 25 rnds of patt. On rnd 26, turn work and follow patt row 2 back and forth on WS. Cont working patt back and forth for a total of 13 rows.
- On next rnd, join and work 11 more rnds, foll "In the round." BO firmly in knit.

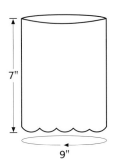

7"

9"

Lucinda Shells Shawl

ROMANTIC AND LACY, this shawl is a cloud of ethereal fluff. Make a smaller one for shoulders, a larger one for dramatic evening wear.

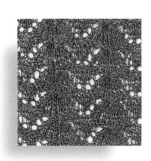

MATERIALS

- Approximately 1000 yards 100% Handspun Angora from Susan Emerson*, color blue, or other lace-weight yarn
- 1 cone Euroflax Lace Weight 14/1 from Louet Sales (3.5 ounces, 5200 yards per cone), color French Blue*, or other lace-weight yarn
- Size 1 (2.5 mm) circular needle (29") or size needed to obtain gauge

Hold one strand of angora and one strand of linen together for entire shawl.

GAUGE

Each shell measures 1¾" wide and ¾" long with one strand of angora and one strand of linen held together.

FINISHED MEASUREMENTS (BLOCKED)

WIDTH: 68"
CENTER BACK LENGTH: 29"

PATTERN STITCH

Multiple of 9 plus 3

Row 1 (RS): K2, *YO, K8, YO, K1*, rep from * to * to last st, K1.
Row 2: K3, *P8, K3*, rep from * to *.
Row 3: K3, *YO, K8, YO, K3*, rep from * to *.
Row 4: K4, *P8, K5*, rep from * to * to last 12 sts, P8, K4.
Row 5: K4, *YO, K8, YO, K5*, rep from * to * to last 12 sts, YO, K8, YO, K4.
Row 6: K5, *P8, K7*, rep from * to * to last 13 sts, P8, K5.
Row 7: K5, *K4tog tbl, K4tog, K7*, rep from * to * to last 13 sts, K4tog tbl, K4tog, K5.

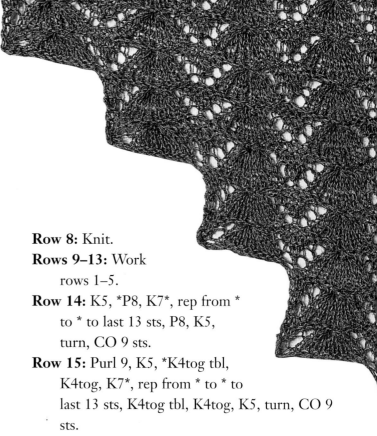

Row 8: Knit.
Rows 9–13: Work rows 1–5.
Row 14: K5, *P8, K7*, rep from * to * to last 13 sts, P8, K5, turn, CO 9 sts.
Row 15: Purl 9, K5, *K4tog tbl, K4tog, K7*, rep from * to * to last 13 sts, K4tog tbl, K4tog, K5, turn, CO 9 sts.
Row 16: Knit.

SHAWL

CO 12 sts. Knit 1 row.
Work the following 16 rows once to start the shawl.
Row 1 (RS): K2, YO, K8, YO, K2.
Row 2: K3, P8, K3.
Row 3: K3, YO, K8, YO, K3.
Row 4: K4, P8, K4.
Row 5: K4, YO, K8, YO, K4.
Row 6: K5, P8, K5.
Row 7: K5, K4tog tbl, K4tog, K5.
Row 8: Knit.
Rows 9–13: Rep rows 1–5.
Row 14: Work as for row 6, CO 9 sts at end of row.
Row 15: P9, work as for row 7, CO 9 sts at end of row.
Row 16: Knit—30 sts.

- Rem shawl is worked in 16-row patt-st rep. Work until there are 35 shells across, ending with a completed row 13. Work rows 14–16 as foll:

Row 14: K5, *P8, K7*, rep from * to * to last 13 sts, P8, K5.

Row 15: Purl 9, K5, *K4tog tbl, K4tog, K7*, rep from * to * to last 13 sts, K4tog tbl, K4tog, K5.

Row 16: Knit—318 sts.

- Knit 2 rows, BO in picot as foll: BO 2 sts, *sl rem st on RH needle to LH needle and CO 2 sts, BO 4 sts*, rep from * to *.

FINISHING

Even though this shawl is 50% angora and 50% linen, it must be washed as if it were 100% angora. See page 133 for angora washing instructions.

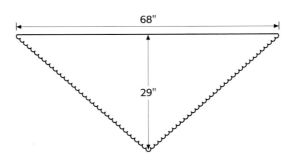

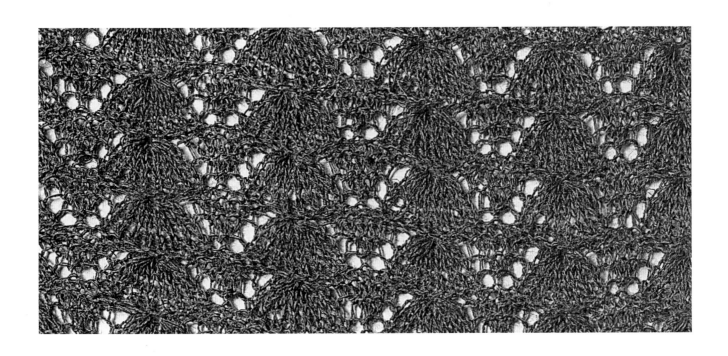

Qiviut

Musk Ox (Photo by John Nash)

PRONOUNCED KEE-VEE-UTE— and one of the few words in the dictionary that doesn't have a *u* after the *q*—qiviut is most likely the softest stuff on the face of the earth. It comes from the musk ox, an animal that has changed little since prehistoric times.

During the 1800s and early 1900s, these animals were hunted almost to extinction. In 1917 a law went into effect to protect the beasts, and while still rare, they now live mainly in the Arctic areas of Canada, Greenland, and Alaska. The worldwide population is estimated now at about 100,000. An adult male can measure 4 to 5 feet at the shoulders and weigh as much as 900 pounds, with massive horns that they use for fighting during mating season. Two males will charge at each other, head on, and collide, the clashing sound of the impact ringing across the tundra. The males have a gland under their eyes that they use for marking territory. It leaves a musky odor, hence their name. When threatened, the herd will form a formidable circle with horns facing outward.

There are limited numbers of people who are willing to raise the animals in captivity. John and Dianne Nash of Palmer, Alaska, are primarily hay farmers who were interested in alternative livestock. Two years ago, they bought three musk oxen and now have a herd of seven. Incredibly, neither one of them was interested in fiber at the time of purchase, but Dianne has since learned to spin and knit.

In summer the oxen graze on pasture grass, and in winter John feeds them grass hay as well as a daily grain supplement. What I really wanted to know about these animals was how the precious fiber was obtained. In the wild it is shed naturally and can be collected from wherever it lands. In order for John to comb his animals he must wait for the approximate time when the shed will occur. The animal is then led to a pen, which leads to a combing cage or squeeze chute. Underneath an incredibly shaggy and unkempt coat of outer guard hair, which can be as much as 16" long, lurks the treasured down of qiviut. Once the musk ox is in the squeeze chute, John takes a coarse-toothed pick and combs the soft underwool from the belly. An average yield is 5 pounds, but once processed and dehaired, it can lose as much as 30% of that weight.

Musk Oxen in Winter (Photo by John Nash)

The natural color of qiviut is a grayish brown, but it accepts dye very well. Eight times warmer than wool and finer than cashmere, one pound of qiviut, spun very finely, would make 6 miles of yarn, and 1950 individual qiviut fibers laid side by side would cover an inch. It is most likely the softest yarn you will ever encounter!

DESIGNING AND KNITTING WITH QIVIUT

BECAUSE of its cost, one tries to make a little bit of qiviut go a long way. Usually small items are made from it, both because the cost is prohibitive, but also because an entire garment knit from qiviut would most likely be much too warm to wear. The one item I offer in this book is the Curry Cockleshell Scarf (page 90). While I used two skeins to make the one shown, I have also written the directions to fashion a smaller-size scarf from just one skein. Everyone should experience the pleasure of knitting with qiviut at least once.

Musk Ox with Calf (Photo by John Nash)

Curry Cockleshell Scarf

WHEN I VISITED SHETLAND, the northernmost islands off the coast of Scotland, I fell in love with the traditional cockleshell pattern that the local women use in the scarves they knit from lace-weight yarn. Almost every shop window on Commercial Street in Lerwick has a variety of these beautiful scarves on display. My version may not use the traditional Shetland materials, but I'm pretty sure most knitters won't object to the luxury of qiviut.

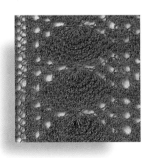

MATERIALS

- 1 (2) skeins Qiviut Fingering Weight from Moco Yarns (100% qiviut; 28 grams, 220 yards per skein), color Curry, or other fingering-weight yarn
- Size 8 (5 mm) needles or size needed to obtain gauge
- Stitch markers
- Stitch holder

GAUGE

17 sts = 4" in pattern stitch

FINISHED MEASUREMENTS (AFTER BLOCKING)

LENGTH: 30 (46)"
WIDTH: 12"

PATTERN STITCH

NOTE: Work the knit into front and back of st in YO from previous row.

Row 1 (RS): YO, K2tog, K1, K2tog, YO, K2, pm, *K1, YO, K2tog, K13, K2tog, YO, K1*, rep from * to * to last 7 sts, pm, K2tog, YO, K5—52 sts.

Row 2: YO, K2tog, K1, K2tog, YO, K2, *K1, knit into front and back of next st, K15, knit into front and back of next st, K1*, rep from * to * to last 7 sts, K2tog, YO, K5—56 sts.

Rows 3 and 4: YO, K2tog, K1, K2tog, YO, K2, knit to last 7 sts, K2tog, YO, K5—56 sts.

Row 5: YO, K2tog, K1, K2tog, YO, K2, *K1, (YO, K2tog) 2 times, K11, (K2tog, YO) 2 times, K1*, rep from * to * to last 7 sts, K2tog, YO, K5—56 sts.

Row 6: YO, K2tog, K1, K2tog, YO, K2, *(K1, knit into front and back of next st) 2 times, K13, (knit into front and back of next st, K1)

2 times*, rep from * to * to last 7 sts, K2tog, YO, K5—64 sts.

Rows 7 and 8: As rows 3 and 4—64 sts.

Row 9: YO, K2tog, K1, K2tog, YO, K2, *K1, (YO, K2tog) 3 times, (YO, K1) 11 times, YO, (K2tog, YO) 3 times, K1* rep from * to * to last 7 sts, K2tog, YO, K5—88 sts.

Row 10 (WS): YO, K2tog, K1, K2tog, YO, K2, *(K1, knit into front and back of next st) 3 times, bring yarn forward, sl next and every alt st onto RH needle (13 sts), AT SAME TIME drop the 12 YO sts from last row. (Make sure you do not drop that last YO! The first st rem on LH needle is a YO.) Put the LH needle through all of these 13 sts, rotate the needle around the sts and purl them, then (knit into the front and back of next st, K1) 3 times*, rep from * to * to last 7 sts, K2tog, YO, K5—52 sts.

Rows 11 and 12: As rows 3 and 4.

SCARF

- **First half:** CO 52 sts. Knit 1 row.
- Work 12-row patt rep 7 (11) times. Place sts on holder.
- **Second half:** Work another piece exactly like first half.

FINISHING

- Graft the two halves tog using St st grafting (see page 128).
- Wash gently; block.

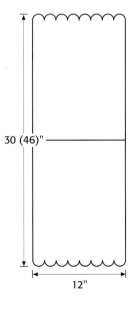

30 (46)"

12"

Cotton

Cotton Plant with Cotton Boll (Photo by Greg Anderson)

THE MOST WIDELY used of all plant fibers, cotton is present is almost every aspect of life today. It is used in clothing, accessories, bedsheets, and household articles. Fibers that are too short to be spun are used in paper and padding, and the oil is used for cooking, soap, cosmetics, and drugs. The remaining parts of the plant are used for livestock feed, fertilizer, and soil conditioners.

Fossilized remains of cotton have been dated to 2900 B.C. As early as 2500 B.C., Peruvian Indians were using cotton to make fishing nets and other items. By 1900 B.C. cotton was being woven, and by 700 B.C. it was successfully being cultivated; by 1500 A.D. it was being used extensively around the world. Easy to grow in hot and humid climates, cotton clothed the masses of the world, with the exception of Europe and Colonial America, where linen remained more popular. By the 1770s, when the American cotton crops began to prosper, cotton finally replaced linen in popularity.

Several inventions spurred the cotton industry. The first was that of the fly shuttle, developed in 1733 by the English inventor John Kay. A mechanical shuttle that replaced the weaver sitting at the loom, it was also the cause of many lost teeth, head injuries, and even death in the weaving mills. Thrown through the shed at high speeds, it often missed its mark, hitting anything in its path. The second invention was that of the spinning jenny, invented by James Hargreaves around 1764, which allowed for several strands of yarn to be spun at once. The machine that changed the course of history and initiated the beginning of the Industrial Revolution, was that of the cotton gin, invented in 1793 by Eli Whitney. Replacing human labor, it separated the seeds from the fiber. With an increased supply of raw materials more readily available, the mills could now churn out cotton at a faster rate. Cotton remained the world's most widely used fiber until the 1950s, when cheap synthetics became popular. By 1977 only about one-third of all fibers used were cotton. Eventually, the synthetics ran their course, and once again cotton regained control of the throne.

Emerging as a seed pod after the cotton flower pollinates itself and drops off, the boll is ready to be picked in about six to nine weeks. In industrialized nations, the harvesting is done by machine; in many undeveloped countries the harvesting is done by hand. The harvest is then put through numerous other pieces of machinery, the cotton gin being one, before it is ready to spin. After the fibers are cleaned and dried, they are compressed and wrapped into bales, each one weighing about 500 pounds. The bales are then classed for quality and sold to a broker. The brokers sell the bales to the spinning mills, where the fiber is made into yarn.

At the mills it is fluffed, cleaned, and carded. It then goes to a machine that produces slivers, or thin ropes. The slivers go through a process called drawing, which makes them thinner and the fibers more parallel, several times. Ready to be spun, the long strands are called roving. The spun yarn, if it is to be used for textiles, goes to the weaving mill. Some cottons are mercerized, a process where the spun yarn is soaked in a strong solution of caustic soda. This changes the fiber structure, making it stronger, easier for the yarn to absorb dye, and giving it a luster.

The two nations that produce the most cotton are China and the United States, with Texas, California, Georgia, and Mississippi being the four leading cotton-producing states. Most of us think of cotton as pure and natural. In the industrialized world, cotton is grown on a huge scale, and this involves industrial farming. Chemicals are added to the soil to kill fungi; insects, the most devastating one being the boll weevil, are controlled by using chemical insecticides; and weeds are reduced by chemical herbicides. Just before harvest, many farmers use a chemical to defoliate the plants, decreasing the amount of plant matter that gets harvested along with the bolls. I live near Willimantic, Connecticut, former home of American Thread. When taking a tour of the now-defunct mills, a story is told of how the Willimantic River was a different color every day of the week, depending on what color the cotton was being dyed that day. Scientists are working daily to develop new plants that are naturally resistant to insects and diseases, and new strains of cotton are being cultivated that are naturally colored.

Designing and Knitting with Cotton

There are rumors about cotton; it shrinks, it's heavy, it has no elasticity, and it stretches. They are all true, to a certain extent, and the designer must take all of these things into consideration. The shrinking factor is easy to control; hand wash only in cold water and do not put into a dryer. Do your measuring with the garment suspended, rather than laid flat. This will take into account, somewhat, any stretch due to weight.

The Sunflower Shell (page 103) was knit from 100% cotton, but because it is just a wispy little thing, the total weight of the garment was not a huge consideration. The smooth texture of the yarn shows off the center panel of lace and leaves the stockinette-stitch sides perfectly smooth.

The lace center panel in the Sunflower Shell provides a pleasing contrast to the smooth stockinette-stitch sides of the shell.

The interplay of yarns creates a wonderful effect in this slip-stitch pattern used in Autumn in New England Pullover.

I loved the Crystal Palace 100% Cotton Chenille that I used for the Autumn in New England Pullover (page 95). I had heard the rumor about chenille worming, so I took into consideration the factors that would keep it from doing this. I knit very firmly on a smaller needle than I would normally use for a yarn of the same diameter, and as an added measure, I chose a slip-stitch pattern, figuring that this would pack in my vertical gauge even tighter.

I had no problems with worming, and the hand-washed sample showed no evidence of shrinkage. The sweater does not weigh a lot and it shows no evidence of growing longer.

The Sage Short-Sleeved Pullover (page 99) is a blend of cotton, silk, and merino. The knitting was a sheer joy. The merino gives the cotton memory, and the silk gives just enough sheen to make it something wonderful.

Autumn in New England Pullover

FALL IS A GLORIOUS TIME of year in New England, when the trees blaze with crimson and yellow and the pines still retain their dark green. The lush green of the cotton chenille makes a velvet background for the tiny bursts of autumn colors created by the slip stitches of the rayon yarn. The body of the sweater is worked in the round up to the armholes, then worked back and forth.

MATERIALS

- 7 (8, 9, 10) skeins Cotton Chenille from Crystal Palace (100% mercerized cotton; 50 grams, 98 yards per skein), color Dark Loden #1903, or other worsted-weight yarn
- 4 (5, 5, 6) skeins Waikiki from Crystal Palace (70% rayon, 30% cotton; 50 grams, 105 yards), color Autumn #2671*, or other sport-weight yarn
- 4 (5, 5, 6) skeins Waikiki from Crystal Palace, color Forest Green Mix #2855*, or other sport-weight yarn
- Two size 4 (3.5 mm) circular needles (16" and 29")
- One set of double-pointed needles, size 4 (3.5 mm)
- Two size 6 (4 mm) circular needles (16" and 29") or size needed to obtain gauge
- One set of double-pointed needles, size 6 (4 mm)
- Stitch markers
- Stitch holders

Both colors of Waikiki are used together throughout entire sweater.

GAUGE

18 sts and 40 rows = 4" in slip-stitch pattern for body on size 6 needles

16 sts and 28 rows = 4" in stockinette stitch for sleeve on size 6 needles

FINISHED MEASUREMENTS

BUST: 38 (42, 46, 50)"

CENTER BACK LENGTH: 19¼ (20½, 22½, 24)"

PATTERN STITCHES

Slip-Stitch Pattern for Body

NOTE: Work sl st wyib on RS rows in the rnd.

In the rnd:

Rnd 1 (RS): With rayon, *K1, sl 1*, rep from * to *.

Rnd 2 (WS): With rayon, *P1, sl 1*, rep from * to *.

Rnds 3 and 4: With chenille, knit.

Rnd 5: With rayon, *sl 1, K1*, rep from * to *.

Rnd 6: With rayon, *sl 1, P1*, rep from * to *.

Rnds 7 and 8: With chenille, knit.

Back and forth:

NOTE: Work sl st wyib on RS rows and wyif on WS rows.

Rows 1 (RS) and 2 (WS): With rayon, *K1, sl 1*, rep from * to *.

Row 3: With chenille, knit.

Row 4: With chenille, purl.

Rows 5 and 6: With rayon, * sl 1, K1*, rep from * to *.

Row 7: With chenille, knit.

Row 8: With chenille, purl.

Seed Stitch

Worked in the rnd or back and forth:

Row 1: *K1, P1*, rep from * to *.

Row 2: Purl the knit sts and knit the purl sts.

Stockinette Stitch for Sleeve

In the rnd:

Rnds 1 and 2: With chenille, knit.

Rnds 3 and 4: With rayon, knit.

Back and forth:

Row 1: With chenille, knit.

Row 2: With chenille, purl.

Row 3: With rayon, knit.

Row 4: With rayon, purl.

FRONT

Border

- **First piece:** With 29" size 4 needle and chenille, loosely CO 84 (92, 102, 110) sts. Work in seed stitch for 12 rows. Break yarn; set aside on a spare needle.
- **Second piece:** Work as for first piece but do not break yarn.
- **To join:** With yarn already attached to second piece, knit across row of second piece, CO 1 st, pm, CO 1 st, knit across row of first piece, CO 1 st, pm, CO 1 st. The markers divide the work into front and back—86 (94, 104, 112) sts each for front and back—172 (188, 208, 224) sts total.

Body

- Change to 29" size 6 needle and knit 1 rnd.
- Work in sl-st patt until piece measures 11 (12, 13, 14)" including border, ending with either a completed rnd 2 or 6.
- Divide for armholes (patt row 3 or 7): Knit to 7 (7, 8, 9) sts before end of rnd, BO 7 (7, 8, 9) sts. At beg of next rnd (4 or 8), BO 8 (8, 9, 10) sts, work to 7 (7, 8, 9) sts before next marker, BO next 15 (15, 17, 19) sts. Work to end of rnd. Break yarn. Front and back are now worked back and forth on 71 (79, 87, 93) sts. Place 1 set of sts on spare needle or holder.
- **Front:** With RS facing, attach yarn. Beg on this row, dec 1 st at each side of armholes every 5 rows 7 (8, 9, 10) times—57 (63, 69, 73) sts.
- Work even until 5¾ (6, 6½, 7)" from armholes, ending with a completed WS row.
- **Shape neck:** Work 20 (22, 24, 25) sts, work middle 17 (19, 21, 23) sts, place on holder, work rem 20 (22, 24, 25) sts. Work each side separately.

- **Right side:** Work WS row. Beg on next row, dec 1 st at neck edge every 5 rows 4 (4, 5, 5) times—16 (18, 19, 20) sts. Work 4 rows even.
- **Shape shoulders:** At beg of next 3 WS rows, BO as foll: 5 (6, 6, 7) sts, 5 (6, 6, 7) sts, and 6 (6, 7, 6) sts.
- **Left side:** Attach yarn at neck edge and work WS row. Work dec as for right side, work 3 rows even. At beg of next 3 RS rows, BO for shoulder shaping as for right side.

BACK

- Work as for front, omitting neck shaping, until piece measures exactly the same to beg of shoulder shaping.
- **Shape shoulders and back neck:** Work 18 (20, 21, 22) sts, work middle 21 (23, 27, 29) sts, place on holder, work rem 18 (20, 21, 22) sts. Work each side separately.
- **Left side:** At beg of next 3 WS rows, BO as foll: 5 (6, 6, 7) sts, 5 (6, 6, 7) sts, and 6 (6, 7, 6) sts, and AT SAME TIME dec 1 st at neck edge on next 2 RS rows.
- **Right side:** Attach yarn and work WS row. Work as for left side, BO shoulder sts on RS rows.

NECKBAND

- Sew shoulder seams.
- With RS facing, 16" size 4 circ needle, and chenille, PU 4 sts down right back, K23 (29, 29, 33) sts from back neck holder, PU 4 sts up left back, PU 13 (13, 15, 15) sts down left front, K17 (19, 21, 23) sts from front neck holder, PU 14 (14, 16, 16) sts up right front, pm—75 (83, 89, 95) sts.
- Work 6 rnds of seed stitch. BO very loosely in patt.

Sleeves

- With size 4 dpn and chenille, very loosely CO 35 (37, 39, 41) sts. Join rnd and pm.

- Work in seed st for 12 rnds, marking off last st of rnd as underarm st. All inc are done on each side of this st as foll: Knit into front and back of first st of rnd, work to 1 st before marker, knit into front and back of st, work st between markers.

- Change to size 6 dpn and sleeve patt, inc 5 (6, 7, 8) sts evenly spaced on first rnd—40 (43, 46, 49) sts. Inc 1 st on each side of underarm stitch every 6 rnds 17 (18, 19, 20) times—74 (79, 84, 89) sts. Work 10 rnds even.

NOTE: Change to 16" size 6 circ, if desired, when there are enough stitches to work comfortably.

- **Shape cap:** BO first 7 (7, 8, 9) sts of rnd, work to end of rnd. Turn work and BO first 8 (8, 9, 10) sts, purl to end of rnd. Working back and forth (see note below), dec 1 st at each side every RS row 7 (8, 9, 10) times. Work WS row. Work 3 rows. Beg on next row, dec 1 st at each side every 4 rows 3 times—39 (42, 43, 44) sts. Work 2 rows even. BO 2 sts at beg of next 8 rows. BO rem 23 (26, 27, 28) sts.

NOTE: It is easier to work back and forth on the sleeve cap if you use one 16" and one 29" circular needle. Work off of one needle onto another. When there is enough ease in the cap shaping, you can resume with just one needle, working back and forth.

Finishing

Sew a sleeve into each armhole.

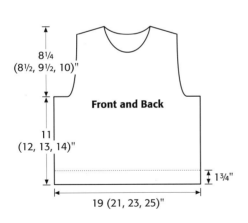

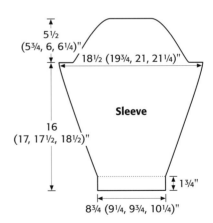

Sage Short-Sleeved Pullover

You won't believe the hand on this luxurious yarn! The little bit of merino gives it spring, the silk gives it sheen, and the cotton gives it comfort. The little cables snug up the fit to body-hugging perfection. If a looser fit is desired, steaming the cables will open them up a bit.

MATERIALS

- 6 (7, 8, 9) skeins Hand Dyed Exotics (4/8 sport weight) from Haneke (65% pima cotton, 15% silk, 20% merino wool; 46 grams, 120 yards per skein), color Dark Lichen, or other sport-weight yarn
- Small amount of waste yarn for provisional CO
- Size 2 (3 mm) circular needle (24")
- One set of double-pointed needles, size 2 (3 mm)
- Size 5 (3.75 mm) circular needle (24") or size needed to obtain gauge
- One set of double-pointed needles, size 5 (3.75)
- Size D/3 (3 mm) crochet hook
- Stitch markers
- Stitch holders

GAUGE

20 sts and 28 rows = 4" in pattern stitch on size 5 needles

FINISHED MEASUREMENTS

BUST: 34 (38, 42, 46)" (Fabric has quite a bit of lateral stretch.)
CENTER BACK LENGTH: 19 (19¾, 20½, 21½)"

LACE PATTERN STITCH

Multiple of 6 plus 1

In the rnd:
Rnds 1, 3, and 5: P1, *K5, P1*, rep from * to *.
Rnd 2: P1, *K1, YO, sl 1, K2tog, psso, YO, K1, P1*, rep from * to *.
Rnd 4: P1, *K2, YO, SSK, K1, P1*, rep from * to *.
Rnd 6: P1, *K5, P1*, rep from * to *.
Rep rnds 1–6 for patt.

Back and forth:
Rows 1, 3, and 5 (WS): K1, *P5, K1*, rep from * to *.
Rows 2, 4, and 6: Work same as in the rnd.

BODY

The body is worked in the rnd up to the armholes, then worked back and forth.

- **Hem:** With size 2 circ needle, crochet hook, and waste yarn, provisionally CO 95 (107, 119, 131) sts for front (see page 126), pm, and 95 (107, 119, 131) sts for back—190 (214, 238, 262) sts. Join, pm.
- Work hem patt as foll for 10 rnds: (K2, *P1, K5*, rep from * to * to 2 sts before marker, K2) 2 times. Purl 1 rnd for turning.
- Change to size 5 circ needle and work 8 rnds of hem patt.
- **Turn hem:** Carefully pull out provisional CO and place live sts on size 2 needle. Holding this needle behind the size 5 needle, work sts from both needles tog in hem patt.
- Beg lace patt st, keeping 2 sts on either side of each marker in St st. Dec 1 st at each side of markers when work measures 3 (3, 3½, 3¾)" and 4 (4, 4½, 4¾)"—182 (206, 230, 254) sts. Inc 1 st at each side of markers when work measures 5 (5, 5½, 5¾)" and 6 (6, 6½, 6¾)"—190 (214, 238, 262) sts.
- Work even until entire piece measures 11½ (12, 12½, 13)", ending with a completed even-numbered rnd.
- **Divide for armholes (odd-numbered rnd):** Work to 6 (7, 8, 9) sts before end of rnd, BO 6 (7, 8, 9) sts. At beg of next rnd (even-numbered rnd), BO 6 (7, 8, 9) sts, work to next marker, BO next 12 (14, 16, 18) sts, work to end of rnd—83 (93, 103, 113) sts each for front and back. Now work back and forth. Place the 83 (93, 103, 113) sts of back on holder.

FRONT

NOTE: Keep any partial 5-st lace patt in St st.

- **Shape armholes:** Work WS row. Dec 1 st at each side every RS row 6 (7, 8, 9) times— 71 (79, 87, 95) sts.
- Work even until armhole measures 5¾ (6, 6½ , 7)", ending with a completed WS row.
- **Shape front neck:** Work 28 (31, 34, 37) sts, place next 15 (17, 19, 21) sts on holder for front neck. Work each side separately.
- **Left side:** BO 2 sts at beg of next 3 WS rows, then dec 1 st at neck edge every WS row 4 (5, 6, 7) times—18 (20, 22, 24) sts. Work even until armhole measures 7½ (7¾, 8, 8½)". At beg of next 3 RS rows, BO as foll: 6 (7, 7, 8) sts, 6 (7, 7, 8) sts, and 6 (6, 8, 8) sts.
- **Right side:** Attach yarn at neck edge and work as for right side, reversing all shaping.

BACK

NOTE: Keep any partial 5-st lace patt in St st.

- Place sts on needle, attach yarn, work WS row. Shape armholes as for front, disregard front neck shaping. Work even until armholes measure the same as front minus 1 row to shoulder shaping, ending with a completed RS row.
- **Next row (WS):** Work 20 (22, 24, 26) sts, place middle 31 (35, 39, 43) sts on holder for back neck. Work each side separately.
- **Left side:** Shape shoulders as for front and AT SAME TIME dec 1 st at neck edge every WS row 2 times.
- **Right side:** Attach yarn at neck edge on WS and work as for right side, reversing all shaping.

SLEEVES

- With size 2 dpn and waste yarn, provisionally CO 63 (69, 75, 81) sts. Join rnd and pm.
- Work hem patt for 10 rnds as foll: K1, P1, *K5, P1*, rep from * to * to last st, K1.
- Purl 1 rnd. Change to size 5 dpn and work 8 rnds of hem patt.
- Turn hem and attach as for body.
- Establish lace patt as foll: K1, work patt rnd 1 to last st, K1.
- Working in established patt, inc 1 st at beg and end of every 3 rnds 15 times, working extra sts as St st until there are enough to work another patt rep—93 (99, 105, 111) sts.
- Work even until piece measures 7½ (7½, 7¾, 8)", ending with a completed even-numbered rnd.
- **Divide:** Work to last 6 (7, 8, 9) sts of rnd, BO 6 (7, 8, 9) sts—87 (92, 97, 102) sts.
- **Next rnd:** BO first 6 (7, 8, 9) sts of rnd, work to end of rnd—81 (85, 89, 93) sts.
- Cont in patt, working back and forth. Work WS row. Dec 1 st at each side every RS row 6 (7, 8, 9) times—69 (71, 73, 75) sts. Work WS row.
- BO 2 sts at beg of next 18 rows, BO 4 sts at beg of next 6 rows—9 (11, 13, 15) sts. BO rem sts.

FINISHING

- Sew shoulder seams.
- **Neckband:** With RS facing, size 5 dpn, and starting at right shoulder, PU 4 sts down right back, work 31 (35, 39, 43) sts from back holder in established hem patt as foll for your size:
  Size 34: (P1, K5) 5 times, P1.
  Size 38: K2, (P1, K5) 5 times, P1, K2.
  Size 42: K4, (P1, K5) 5 times, P1, K4.
  Size 46: (P1, K5) 7 times, P1.

PU 4 sts up left back, PU 21 (24, 27, 30) sts down left front, work 15 (17, 19, 21) sts from front neck holder in established hem patt as foll for your size:

Size 34: K4, P1, K5, P1, K4.

Size 38: (K5, P1) 2 times, K5.

Size 42: P1, (K5, P1) 3 times.

Size 46: K1, P1, (K5, P1) 3 times, K1.

PU 21 (24, 27, 30) sts up right front—96 (108, 120, 132) sts.

Work the foll rnd for your size 4 (5, 5, 6) times:

Size 34: K4, *P1, K5*, rep from * to * to last 2 sts, P1, K1.

Size 38: *P1, K5*, rep from * to *.

Size 42: K2, *P1, K5*, rep from * to * to last 4 sts, P1, K3.

Size 46: K4 *P1, K5*, rep from * to * to last 2 sts, P1, K1.

Purl 1 rnd, knit 1 rnd.

Next rnd: Knit, dec 10 (11, 12, 13) sts evenly spaced—86 (97, 108, 119) sts. Knit 2 more rnds.

- Turn hem at purl ridge and sew live sts to inside (see page 129).
- Sew sleeves into armholes.

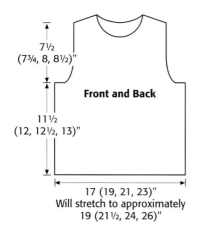

7½ (7¾, 8, 8½)"

Front and Back

11½ (12, 12½, 13)"

17 (19, 21, 23)"
Will stretch to approximately
19 (21½, 24, 26)"

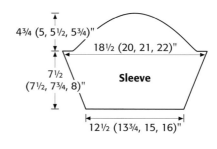

4¾ (5, 5½, 5¾)"

18½ (20, 21, 22)"

7½ (7½, 7¾, 8)"

Sleeve

12½ (13¾, 15, 16)"

Sunflower Shell

SHIMMERY AND LIGHT, this little shell gets its sparkle from mercerization. The smoothness of the yarn gives the center panel incredible relief, which contrasts nicely with the flatness of the stockinette-stitch sides. Other than sewing the side seams and grafting the straps, there is no finishing work to do. The armhole edges and straps roll slightly under to self-finish.

MATERIALS

- 6 (6, 7, 7, 8) skeins Pure Cotton from Jaeger (100% mercerized cotton; 50 grams, 122 yards per skein), color Corn #528, or other DK-weight yarn
- Size 2 (3 mm) needles
- Size 3 (3.25 mm) needles or size needed to obtain gauge
- Stitch marker
- Stitch holder

GAUGE

23 sts and 29 rows= 4" in stockinette stitch on size 3 needles

FINISHED MEASUREMENTS

BUST: 38 (40, 42, 44, 46)"
CENTER BACK LENGTH: 14½ (14½, 15½, 15½, 16½)"

PATTERN STITCH

Stockinette Stitch
Row 1 (RS): Knit.
Row 2 (WS): Purl.

CENTER PANEL (22 STS)

NOTE: Sl all sts pw wyib.
Row 1 and all WS rows: P10, K2, P10.
Row 2 (RS): K6, SSK, return resulting st to LH needle, and with point of RH needle pass next st over it and off needle; then sl st back to RH needle (this is the "SSK and pass" below); YO, K1, YO, P2, YO, K1, YO, sl 1, K2tog, psso, K6.

Row 4: K4, SSK and pass, K1, (YO, K1) twice, P2, K1, (YO, K1) twice, sl 1, K2tog, psso, K4.
Row 6: K2, SSK and pass, K2, YO, K1, YO, K2, P2, K2, YO, K1, YO, K2, sl 1, K2tog, psso, K2.
Row 8: SSK and pass, K3, YO, K1, YO, K3, P2, K3, YO, K1, YO, K3, sl 1, K2tog, psso.

FRONT

- With size 2 needle and using cable-edge cast on (see page 126), CO 110 (116, 122, 128, 134) sts. Purl 5 (5, 5, 7, 7) rows. Change to size 3 needles.
- Establish patt on WS as foll: P42 (45, 48, 51, 54), K2, work row 1 of center panel, K2, P42 (45, 48, 51, 54).
  Next row: K42 (45, 48, 51, 54), P2, work row 2 of center panel, P2, K42 (45, 48, 51, 54).
  Cont in above manner, until 11 (11, 12, 12, 13) rep of center panel have been worked—88 (88, 96, 96, 104) rows. Work row 1 of center panel.
- **Shape armhole:** BO 10 (11, 12, 13, 14) sts at beg of next 2 rows—90 (94, 98, 102, 106) sts.
  Work foll 2 rows a total of 14 times, then work row 1 again—60 (64, 68, 72, 76) sts:
  Row 1 (RS): K3, sl 1, K1, psso, work in patt to last 5 sts, K2tog, K3.
  Row 2 (WS): Work in established patt.
- **Next row (WS):** Working in established patt, work 20 (22, 24, 26, 28) sts, work middle 20 sts and place on holder, work rem 20 (22, 24, 26, 28) sts. Work each side separately.
- **Right armhole and neck:** Cont armhole dec as above, work to last 5 sts, K2tog, K3 (neck dec). Turn work and work WS row. Cont to dec at both armhole edge and neck edge every RS row 5 (6, 7, 8, 9) more

times—8 sts. Work only armhole dec 4 more times—4 sts. Place sts on st marker.

- **Left armhole and neck:** With RS facing, attach yarn at neck edge and work other side to correspond, working neck dec as foll: K3, sl 1 kw, K1, psso.
- **Straps:** Work 4 rem sts of strap in St st for 2". Place sts on st marker. Rep for other strap.

BACK

Work another piece exactly the same as front.

FINISHING

- Sew side seams. Center sts of neck will want to turn under at the curved line of the patt. Carefully sew down live sts to make a hem (see page 129).
- Graft front and back straps at shoulders (see page 128).
- Steam gently, but do not pull down gentle curve of center patt at lower edge. Do not press open St-st straps and armhole shaping, but let them gently roll to form a finished edge.

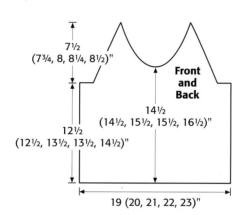

7½
(7¾, 8, 8¼, 8½)"

14½
(14½, 15½, 15½, 16½)"

Front and Back

12½
(12½, 13½, 13½, 14½)"

19 (20, 21, 22, 23)"

Linen and Hemp

Flax Plant Flower (Photo by Masters of Linen)

EMNANTS OF LINEN fabrics over 7000 years old have been found almost perfectly preserved from ancient archeological sites. At this time, the ancient Egyptians were producing linen textiles from the flax crops they grew along the banks of the Nile. Holding it in great esteem, they wrapped their mummies in it. During the 1600s the skilled artisans of northern Europe brought the spinning and weaving of linen to its pinnacle. Since then, the countries of France, Belgium, and Ireland have remained famous for their fine linen, since these countries have a climate that is ideally suited for its cultivation. In the 1640s the colonies of Massachusetts and Connecticut required every family to raise flax or hemp. It was of great importance to the early settlers, because it allowed them to replace clothing and household necessities that had been brought with them from England.

Before the invention of Eli Whitney's cotton gin in 1793, linen was the most important vegetable fiber used for textiles in Europe and America. During the Middle Ages only nobility could afford to wear linen; in Colonial America white linen clothing was reserved for Sunday best. Since linen has been extensively used for bedsheets, tablecloths, napkins, dish towels, and handkerchiefs throughout history, the term *linens* has become a generic name for all of the above.

The terms *linen* and *flax* are sometimes used interchangeably. Technically, linen is the product that is made from the fibers of the flax plant. Incredibly long, these fibers can range from 6" to 40" in length and come from the stem of the plant. A fast-growing plant, flax takes only about 100 days to mature.

Field of Flax Plants
(Photo by Masters of Linen)

The plants are harvested by machines that pull them from the ground and lay the stalks parallel to each other. They are then left on the ground for the retting process, a natural process of decomposition which breaks down the material that surrounds the fibers, allowing the fiber to be more easily separated from the stalk. After the retting process, flax is dried and compacted into bales. Dried flax is highly flammable, and in the past, many villages were lost due to flax fires.

In a process called skutching, the dried flax is pounded and beaten to separate the fibers from any remaining stalk material. The next step is hackling, in which the fibers are raked to untangle them and lay them all parallel. From this process, the short fibers, called tow, are separated from the longer fibers, called line. Line is softer and used for high-quality products, while the tow is coarser and used for less expensive items. The next process is drafting, in which the fibers are made ready for spinning by drawing them into roves. The final step, spinning, can be done either wet, dry, or semi-wet. Many philosophers have compared the sufferings of mankind to the tortures that flax must undergo before it becomes linen!

Like the flax plant, hemp is grown for the use of its strong fiber, which was once used extensively for rope, cord, and twine.

Hemp was also widely used around the world for clothing throughout history and is still popular today. It is basically a weed that will thrive in  almost any part of the world and can be successfully cultivated without the use of chemicals and pesticides. The cultivation of it is illegal in the United States—the dried leaves and flowers of a different variety of this plant are the source of marijuana. Hemp is processed for fiber much the same way as linen.

Hemp Plant
(Photo by Greg Anderson)

Because linen and hemp are derived from a plant, they are termed cellulose fibers, as opposed to fibers that are termed protein fibers. Each type of fiber must use a different type of dye and dye process to take on color. Louet Sales carries their same color line in both merino yarn and 100% linen yarn. It is interesting to notice how each fiber takes the same color dye a little differently. The linen also has a discernable sheen to it.

Lana Hames, of Lanaknits, sells 100% hemp. Her colors are vibrant and saturated because she uses a fiber-reactive dye specifically for cellulose fiber. The colors are permanent and resist fading. If she wants a light shade, she soaks the yarn in a solution of hydrogen peroxide and water. Her skeins are all prewashed and soaked in an industrial fabric-softener solution for a softer hand and more enjoyable knitting experience.

Both linen and hemp benefit from being washed—the more, the better. Each time it is washed it becomes softer and more pliable. Lana says she put the first hemp sweater she ever knit into a washer and agitated it for hours on end. It emerged as soft as butter.

Hemp Fiber Ready to Spin (Left) and Finished Product

Both fibers are easier to spin when they are wet. It is interesting to note that in the traditional method of hand spinning, saliva was used as the source of moisture. You may remember, it was "an old woman with a spindle, diligently spinning her flax" that led Sleeping Beauty to try her hand at spinning. When she pricked her finger upon the spindle, a series of unfortunate events arose to fulfill an evil prophecy that had been declared at her birth.

Designing with Linen and Hemp

My main concern in designing and knitting with these fibers is the general lack of elasticity in the 100% varieties. Lana Hames warns that hemp stretches after wear, but gives careful gauge information on her labels for before and after washing. Certainly, the prudent designer can take measures to ensure the gauge is correct so this won't be a problem. But being just a slight bit chicken, I took the easy way out with the 100% hemp and designed the colorful and fun Striped Market Bag (page 120). I wanted something sturdy, so I chose to knit garter stitch. The delightfully vibrant colors were enough to buoy my spirits on even the grayest of New England winter days, and I dreamed of warm sand beaches and bright sunlight as I was knitting.

Trudy van Stralen, president of Louet Sales, first convinced me to try knitting with linen. She assured me I could throw the finished garment into the washer (yes, in hot water!) and then into the dryer (yes, on heat!). I found I could not knit in my usual style of carrying the yarn in my left hand, since I just couldn't get enough tension to satisfy me. I switched to my old way of carrying yarn in my right hand, and this worked better. I must admit that I had a wonderful time knitting the Willow Linen Pullover (page 117). With great trepidation I followed Trudy's advice on washing and drying. I held my breath when I reached into the dryer to retrieve the finished product, following Trudy's tip to take it out while it was still slightly wet and then lay it flat to finish the drying process. I was ecstatic when I pulled the garment from the dryer. It was soft and drapey with the same beautiful sheen, and it hadn't shrunk a single centimeter. As knitters, we have been so conditioned over the years to assume that anything we make and put in the dryer will automatically come out ruined! Now we must recondition ourselves to believe that if we don't put our linen items in the washer and dryer we are doing the fiber a great disservice.

Hemp yarn produces a strong, well-defined stitch in the Striped Market Bag.

Unwashed Linen (Left) and Washed, Dried, and Pressed Linen

When working with 100% linen or hemp, it is a good idea to avoid ribbing, because it has a tendency to stretch out of shape after washing. Trudy also mentions that plain stockinette stitch has a tendency to skew and recommends that you break up large areas with other stitches.

When blended with wool and other fibers, the nonelastic properties of linen and hemp are totally overcome. Kathy Haneke's sumptuous blend of linen, alpaca, and merino in the Haneke Red Pullover (page 110) was a total delight to work with. The crispness of the linen gave the yarn the perfect stitch definition I wanted for the traveling stitches that make up the design. The alpaca and merino impart the luxury and softness.

The linen content of this yarn provides just the right amount of crispness for beautiful stitch definition in the Haneke Red Pullover.

Haneke Red Pullover

KATHY HANEKE IS A
blending genius. In this
yarn she combines the
crispness of linen with
the luxury and softness of
alpaca and merino. The
color is something that
needs no improvement.
All together, I never wanted
this knitting to end.

Materials

- 10 (11, 12) skeins Haneke Exotics from Haneke Wool Fashions (35% linen, 30% baby alpaca, 35% merino wool; 50 grams, 147 yards per skein), color Red #6085, or other sport-weight yarn
- Two size 5 (3.75 mm) circular needles (16" and 29") or size needed to obtain gauge
- One set of double-pointed needles, size 5 (3.75 mm)
- Stitch markers
- Stitch holders

Gauge

24 sts and 32 rows = 4" in stockinette stitch on size 5 needles

Finished Measurements

BUST: 40 (44½, 49)"
CENTER BACK LENGTH: 24 (26½, 29)"

Pattern Stitch

Right and Left Twists (see page 127) are worked on RS rows only.
WS Rows: In the rnd, knit; back and forth, purl.

Front and Back Border

- With 29" circ needle, CO 120 (134, 148) sts. Work foll row 6 times: sl first st wyib, purl to end of row.
- Work 48 rows of Chart A (border). Break yarn and set aside on a spare needle.
- Make another piece exactly the same but do not break yarn.
- **Join borders:** With yarn that is attached, purl across sts of second border piece, pm, purl across sts of first border piece, pm—240 (268, 296) sts.
- Knit 1 row, purl 1 row, knit 1 row.

Body

The body is worked in the rnd up to the armholes, then worked back and forth.
NOTE: Only the RS rows of pattern are shown on charts. They are designated as odd-numbered rows. All alternate rows are even-numbered rows and are worked in pattern stitch.

- Establish patt as foll: *Work 24 (31, 38) sts of RH side of Chart C in your size, work 72 sts of Chart B (body), work 24 (31, 38) sts of LH side of Chart C.* For front, rep from * to * as for back.
- Cont in established patt until entire piece measures 16 (18, 20)".
- **Divide for armholes:** Cont in patt, *work to 6 (8, 8) sts before marker, BO next 12 (16, 16) sts*, rep from * to *. Break yarn. Place 108 (118, 132) sts of back on holder. Sweater is now worked by knitting back and forth.

Front

- Attach yarn to WS of front sts and work alternate row.
- **Shape armholes:** Keeping first 2 sts and last 2 sts in St st, dec 1 st at each armhole edge every RS row 8 (10, 12) times—92 (98, 108) sts.
- Work even in patt until armhole measures 6", ending with a completed WS row.
- **Shape front neck:** Work 40 (42, 46) sts, work middle 12 (14, 16) sts and place on holder, work rem 40 (42, 46) sts. Work each side separately.
- **Right side:** Work alternate row. BO 2 sts at beg of next 2 RS rows, then dec 1 st at neck edge every RS row 5 (6, 7) times—31 (32, 35) sts.
- Work even until armhole measures 8 (8½, 9)".
- **Shape shoulders:** At beg of next 3 WS rows, BO as foll: 10 (11, 12) sts, 10 (11, 12) sts, and 11 (10, 11) sts.

- **Left side:** Attach yarn at neck edge on WS and work as for right side, working decs on WS, and shoulder BO on RS.

BACK

- Attach yarn to WS of back sts and work alternate row.
- Shape armholes as for front, work even until armhole measures 8 (8½, 9)", ending with a completed WS row.
- **Shape back neck:** Work 35 (36, 39) sts, work middle 22 (26, 30) sts and place on holder, work rem 35 (36, 39) sts. Work each side separately.
- **Left side:** At beg of next 2 WS rows, BO as for front and AT SAME TIME dec 1 st at neck edge every row 4 times. BO rem sts.
- **Right side:** Attach yarn at neck edge on WS. Work as for left side but work dec and BO on RS rows.

NECKBAND

- With RS facing, 16" circ needle, and starting at right shoulder, PU 6 sts down right back, K22 (26, 30) sts from back neck holder, PU 6 sts up left back, PU 15 (17, 19) sts down left front, K12 (14, 16) sts from holder, PU 15 (17, 19) sts up right front, pm—76 (86, 96) sts.
- (Purl 1 rnd, knit 1 rnd) 2 times, purl 1 rnd. Turn work, BO in knit from WS.
- Fasten off and use short tail of yarn to weave both little sides of neckband tog.

SLEEVES

NOTE: Only the right-side rows of pattern are shown on charts. They are designated as odd-numbered rows. All alternate rows are even-numbered rows and are worked in the pattern stitch.

- With dpn, CO 46 (56, 60) sts. Join rnd.
- (Purl 1 rnd, knit 1 rnd) 3 times. Establish patt from Chart D as foll: For sizes Small and Large, work brackets as indicated. For size Medium, work 5 sts of RH extension, work middle 46 sts of size Small, work 5 sts of LH extension.
- Work even in patt through rnd 10 (alternate row not shown on chart) of Chart D. Beg on next rnd, inc 1 st at beg and end of rnd every 4 rnds 4 times—54 (64, 68) sts. Incorporate extra sts into St st patt.
- Work even through rnd 32 (alternate rnd not shown on chart) of Chart D.
- Purl 1 rnd, knit 1 rnd, purl 1 rnd.
- Rest of sleeve is worked in St st; change to 16" circ needle when necessary. Inc 1 st at beg and end of rnds as foll: next rnd and every 3 rnds 5 times, every 4 rnds 3 times, every 5 rnds 2 times, every 6 rnds 11 times—96 (106, 110) sts. Work even for 2 (6, 8) rnds.
- **Divide for sleeve cap:** Work to 6 (8, 8) sts before end of next rnd, BO 6 (8, 8) sts at end of this rnd and 6 (8, 8) sts at beg of next rnd—84 (90, 94) sts. Work to end of rnd. Sleeve cap is now worked back and forth. Work WS row.
- Dec 1 st at each side on next 13 (15, 17) RS rows—58 (60, 60) sts.
- BO 2 sts at beg of next 6 rows—46 (48, 48) sts.
- BO 9 sts at beg of next 4 rows. BO rem 10 (12, 12) sts.

FINISHING

- Sew sleeves into armholes.
- Steam very lightly but do not press iron over texture work.

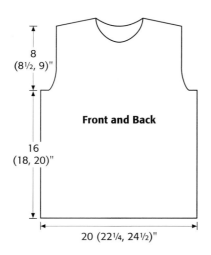

Front and Back

8
(8½, 9)"

16
(18, 20)"

20 (22¼, 24½)"

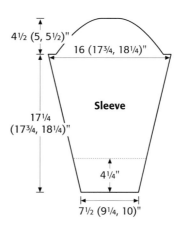

Sleeve

4½ (5, 5½)"

16 (17¾, 18¼)"

17¼
(17¾, 18¼)"

4¼"

7½ (9¼, 10)"

Chart A
Border

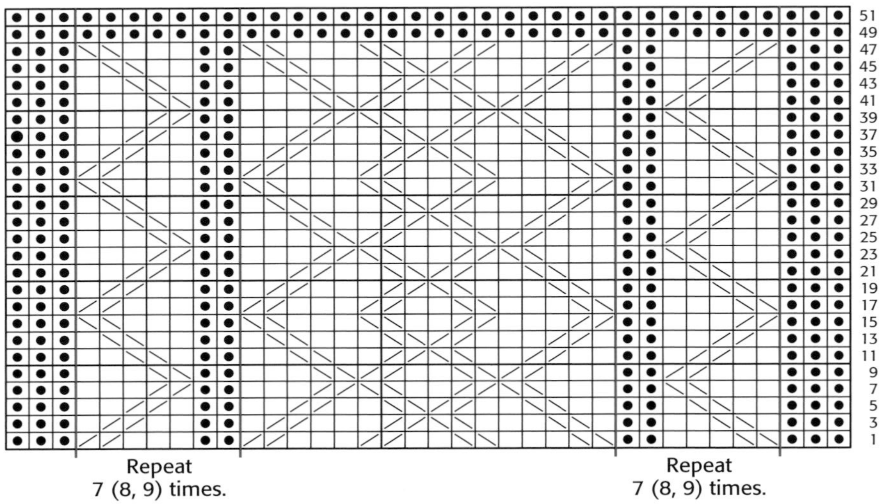

Repeat
7 (8, 9) times.

Repeat
7 (8, 9) times.

51 49 47 45 43 41 39 37 35 33 31 29 27 25 23 21 19 17 15 13 11 9 7 5 3 1

Chart B
Body

35 33

31 29 27 25 23 21 19 17 15 13 11 9 7 5 3 1

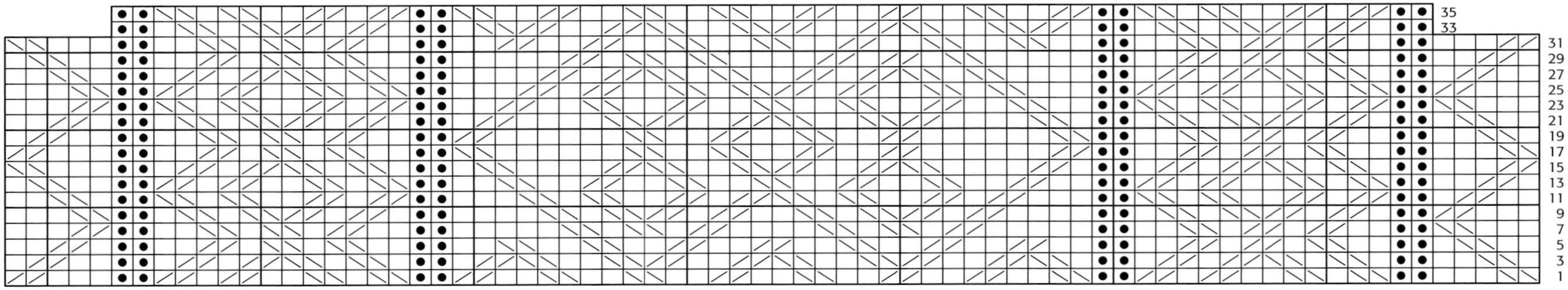

Key

St st

Left Twist (LT)

Right Twist (RT)

● Purl

Chart C
Sides Size Small

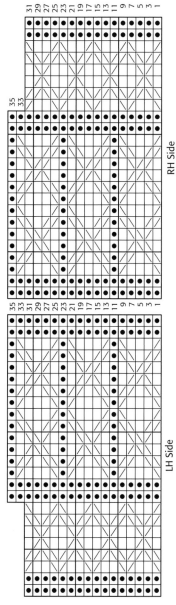

RH Side

LH Side

Chart C
Sides Size Medium

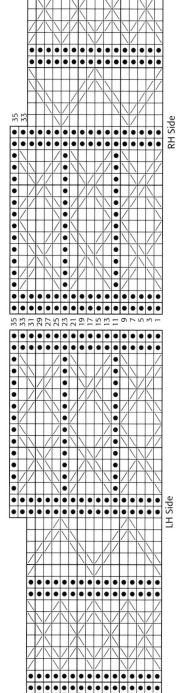

RH Side

LH Side

Key
☐ St st
◪ Left Twist (LT)
◪ Right Twist (RT)
● Purl

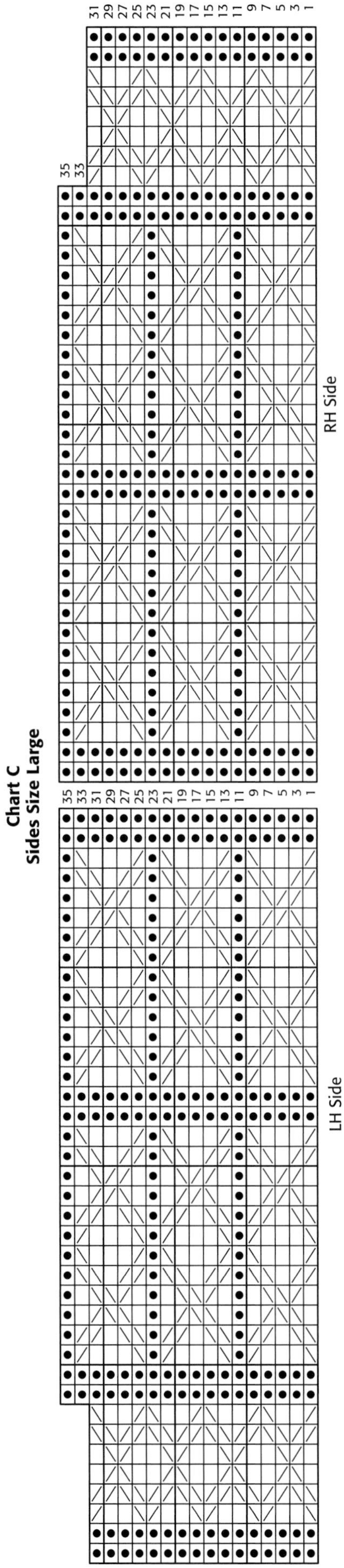
Chart C
Sides Size Large
RH Side
LH Side
1 3 5 7 9 11 13 15 17 19 21 23 25 27 29 31 33 35

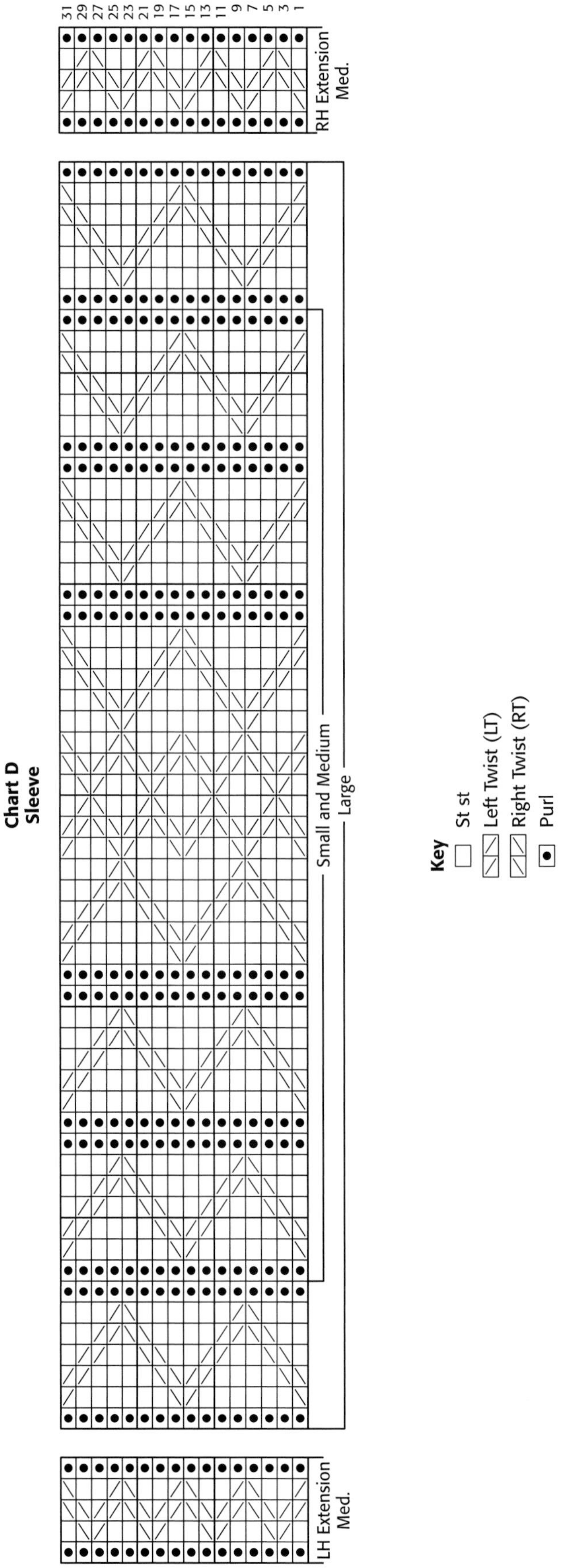
Chart D
Sleeve
RH Extension Med.
LH Extension Med.
Small and Medium
Large
1 3 5 7 9 11 13 15 17 19 21 23 25 27 29 31
Key
St st
Left Twist (LT)
Right Twist (RT)
Purl

Willow Linen Pullover

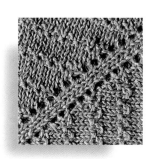

MATERIALS

- 3 (3, 4, 4, 5, 5, 6, 6) skeins Euroflax Sport Weight 14/4 from Louet Sales (100% linen; 100 grams, 285 yards per skein), color Willow, or other sport-weight yarn
- Small amount of waste yarn for provisional CO
- Two size 2 (3 mm) circular needles (16" and 29")
- One long 14" size 2 (3 mm) straight needle
- Two size 3 (3.25 mm) circular needles (16" and 29") or size needed to obtain gauge
- Size D/3 (3 mm) crochet hook
- Stitch markers (2 different colors)
- Stitch holder

GAUGE

22 sts and 28 rows = 4" in pattern stitch on size 3 needles

FINISHED MEASUREMENTS

Bust: 38½ (40¾, 42, 44¼, 46½, 48¾, 50, 52¼)"
Center Back Length: 18½ (19½, 20½, 21½, 22½, 23½, 24½, 25½)"

PATTERN STITCH

Rows 1–4: Knit.
Row 5: *P1, K1*, rep from * to * until sts are used up.
Row 6: *Knit the purl sts, purl the knit sts*, rep from * to * until sts are used up.

BODY

- **Neck hem:** With size 2 straight needle, crochet hook, and waste yarn, provisionally CO 100 (100, 104, 108, 112, 116, 120, 124) sts (see page 126). With linen, knit sts onto 16" size 2 circ needle, pm of a different color other than that which will be used later in the pattern. Knit 3 more rnds for hem. Purl one rnd for turning.
- Change to 16" size 3 needle and work patt as foll:
  Rnd 1: Sl marker, work in patt 35 (35, 37, 39, 41, 43, 45, 47) sts for back, pm, 15 sts for sleeve, pm, 35 (35, 37, 39, 41, 43, 45, 47) sts for front, pm, 15 sts for sleeve.
  Rnd 2 (inc rnd): *K1, YO, work in patt to 1 st before next marker, YO, K1, sl marker*; rep from * to * 3 more times (8 sts increased).
  Rnd 3: Work even in patt.
  Rnd 4: Work inc rnd in patt.
  Rnd 5: *K1, work in patt to 1 st before next marker, K1*, rep from * to * around rnd.
  Rnd 6: Work inc rnd in patt.
  Rep rnds 1–6 until a total of 33 (36, 37, 39, 41, 43, 44, 46) inc rnds have been worked or when desired armhole length is reached, changing to longer needle when necessary—364 (388, 400, 420, 440, 460, 472, 492) sts.
- **Divide for armholes:** Remove all markers as you work this rnd. CO 2 sts, work 101 (107, 111, 117, 123, 129, 133, 139) sts of back, *sl 81 (87, 89, 93, 97, 101, 103, 107) sts for sleeve to holder*, CO 5 sts for underarm, work 101 (107, 111, 117, 123, 129, 133, 139) sts of front, rep from * to *, CO 3 sts, pm. Work even on 212 (224, 232, 244, 256, 268, 276, 288) sts until piece measures 11 (11½, 12, 12½, 13, 13½, 14, 14½)" or until desired length from underarm, ending with a completed rnd 4 of patt. Purl 1 rnd for hem turning. Knit 1 rnd. Knit 1 rnd, dec 21 (22, 23, 24, 25, 26, 27, 28) sts evenly spaced. Knit 2 more rnds. Leave sts on needle.

SLEEVES

- Sl sleeve sts to 16" size 3 circ needle. PU 2 sts from underarm CO sts, work sleeve sts in patt, PU 2 sts from underarm CO sts, pm, PU 1 st, pm—86 (92, 94, 98, 102, 106, 108, 112) sts.
- Work as foll:
  Rnd 1 (dec rnd): K2tog, work to 2 sts before marker, sl 1, K1, psso, sl marker, K1.
  Rnds 2 and 3: Work even.
  Rep above 3 rnds a total of 9 (10, 11, 12, 13, 14, 15, 16) times—68 (72, 72, 74, 76, 78, 78, 80) sts.
- Work even until sleeve measures 4½ (5, 5½, 6, 6½, 7, 7½, 8)" or until desired length, ending with a completed rnd 4 of patt.

- **Sleeve hem:** Purl 1 rnd for hem turning. Knit 1 rnd. Knit 1 rnd, dec 7 (7, 7, 7, 8, 8, 8, 8) sts evenly spaced. Knit 2 more rnds. Place sts on holder.

FINISHING

- **Body and sleeve hems:** Turn hem at purl rnd and carefully slipstitch hem in place, using live sts (see page 129).
- **Neck hem:** Carefully pull out waste yarn from provisional sts. Turn hem at purl rnd and slipstitch hem in place using the live sts.
- Wash in machine with hot water and mild detergent. Dry in machine with heat. Repeated washing and drying will make your linen garment softer.

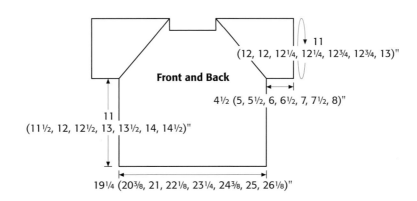

11
(12, 12, 12¼, 12¼, 12¾, 12¾, 13)"

Front and Back

4½ (5, 5½, 6, 6½, 7, 7½, 8)"

11
(11½, 12, 12½, 13, 13½, 14, 14½)"

19¼ (20⅜, 21, 22⅛, 23¼, 24⅜, 25, 26⅛)"

Striped Market Bag

Horizontal Stripes
on Back of Bag

MATERIALS

- Hemp dk Weight from Lanaknits Designs (100% hemp; 50 grams, 93 yards), or other DK-weight yarn, in the following amounts and colors:
  - 3 skeins black
  - 1 skein yellow
  - 1 skein blue
  - 1 skein red
- Small amount of waste yarn for provisional CO
- Size 4 (3.5 mm) needles or size needed to obtain gauge
- Size E/4 (3.5 mm) crochet hook
- Buttons for decoration
- About 3" of Velcro
- Stitch holder

GAUGE

24 sts and 42 rows = 4" in garter stitch on size 4 needles

FINISHED MEASUREMENTS

WIDTH: 12"
HEIGHT: 7"
DEPTH: 3"

PATTERN STITCH

Garter Stitch
Knit every row. (Two rows equal one ridge.)

STRAP

- With black and waste yarn, provisionally CO 17 sts (see page 126). Knit 1 row.
- **Next row:** Sl first st pw wyif, knit to end of row. Rep this row until first skein of black has only about 6" rem. You should have at least 150 ridges. The exact number is not crucial, because you will be finishing the strap later for a custom length. Place sts on holder.
- Fold strap in half and mark center sl st of long side with a piece of colored thread—point A. Count 30 sl sts to the right from center and place a colored thread in the 30th sl st—point B. Do the same to the left of center—point C. Count 40 sl sts to the right from point B and put a colored thread in 40th st—point D. Count 40 sl sts to the left from point C and put a colored thread in 40th st—point E. Rep marking points A–E on opposite long side of strap.

```
        E       C       A       B       D
Cast ┌─────┬───────┬───────┬───────┬─────┐ Place sts
on row └─────┴───────┴───────┴───────┴─────┘ on holder.
```

BAG FRONT (VERTICAL STRIPES)

- With red and starting at point D, PU 41 sts to point B. Turn work; knit back.
  Row 1: Sl first st wyif pw, knit to 1 st before end, sl 1 st kw, PU 1 st in sl-st edge of strap, psso, turn.
  Row 2: Knit, working first 2 sts firmly, turn. Rep rows 1 and 2 in foll number of ridges and color sequence: 7 red, 3 yellow, 5 blue, 2 black, 1 blue, 3 red, 5 yellow, 3 blue, 1 red, 1 black (center).
  NOTE: When changing color, work last st of last row before color change in new color.
- Work backwards from center ridge to create a mirror image, but work only 6 ridges of very last red sequence. Your last row will be in sl st at point C.
- Leave sts on needle. With a new needle, red, and beg at point E (working toward C), PU 41 sts. Turn and knit back. Line up these two needles and graft tog using St st and red (see page 128).

Bag Back
(Horizontal Stripes)

- With red, beg at point C (working toward B), PU 63 sts. Turn and knit back.
  Row 1 (RS): K62 sts, sl 1 kw wyib, PU 1 st in sl-st edge of strap, psso, turn.
  Row 2 (WS): K62 sts, wyif sl 1 pw, insert RH needle into sl-st edge of strap from back (RS) to front (WS) and purl, psso, turn.
  Work above 2 rows in foll number of ridges and color sequence: 7 red, 3 yellow, 5 blue, 2 black, 1 blue, 2 red, 1 yellow (center).
- Work back in mirror image from center, beg with 2 red. Leave sts on needle.

Flap

- With sts on needle from back, knit 1 row with black. Work the foll row until there are 14 ridges of black:
  Wyif sl 1 pw, knit to end of row.
- **Dec for flap:**
  Row 1: Wyif sl 1 pw, K2tog tbl, knit to last 3 sts, K2tog, K1.
  Row 2: Wyif sl 1 pw, knit to end of row.
  Work above 2 rows with black for 6 ridges, then work foll number of ridges and color sequence: 2 red, 1 black, 1 yellow, 1 black, 2 blue, 1 black. BO from WS in knit.

Finishing

- **Strap:** Place sts from holder onto needle and cont working strap for desired length. Carefully pull out provisional CO from other end of strap and graft the two pieces tog (see page 128).
- **Front of bag:** Work around front of bag as follows: With black and starting at RH side, work 1 sc in each sl st. Break thread and fasten off.
- **Flap:** Beg at RH side of back of bag with black, sc in each sl st. Sew Velcro to desired place on flap, sew buttons as desired for decoration.
- If desired, stiffen inside of bag by cutting cardboard to fit along edges and sides. You may also want to line inside with fabric.

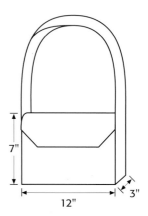

Knitting Abbreviations

beg	beginning
BO	bind off
C4B	back cable (see page 127)
C4F	front cable (see page 127)
CC	contrasting color
ch	chain
circ	circular
cn	cable needle
CO	cast on
cont	continue
dec	decrease
dpn	double-pointed needle
EOR	every other row
foll	follows(ing)
inc	increase
K	knit
K1tbl	knit 1 stitch through back loop
K2tog	knit 2 stitches together
K2tog tbl	knit 2 stitches together through back loop
kw	knitwise
LH	left hand
LT	left twist (see page 127)
M1	make 1 stitch (see page 128)
M1L	make 1 left (see page 128)
M1R	make 1 right (see page 128)
MC	main color
P	purl
P1tbl	purl 1 stitch through back loop

P2tog tbl	purl 2 stitches together through back loop
patt	pattern
pm	place marker
psso	pass slipped stitch(es) over
pw	purlwise
rem	remaining
rep(s)	repeat(s)
rev St st	reverse stockinette stitch
RH	right hand
RT	right twist (see page 127)
rnd(s)	round(s)
RS	right side
sc	single crochet
sl	slip
sl st	slip stitch
SKP	skip 1, knit 1, pass slipped stitch over
SSK	slip, slip, knit 2 stitches together
SSP	slip, slip, purl 2 stitches together
st(s)	stitch(es)
St st	stockinette stitch
tbl	through back loop
tog	together
W and T	wrap and turn
wyib	with yarn in back
wyif	with yarn in front
WS	wrong side
YO	yarn over

Techniques

I AM ASSUMING THAT, as a knitter, you know most of the techniques required to make a sweater. There are a few specific techniques that I call for in individual patterns. These are listed below.

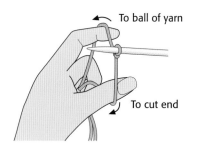

To ball of yarn

To cut end

CASTING ON

CASTING on is a matter of preference. We most likely use the tried-and-true one that we learned when we first learned to knit. If the pattern says to cast on and is not specific, then you may use your favorite method. Some of the patterns in this book, however, call for a specific method. While I cannot stand over you and make you do the called-for method, to get the best results, I strongly recommend you do what I say!

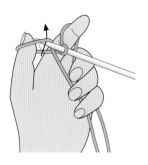

Long-Tail Cast On: Draw out about 1½" of yarn for each stitch to be cast on. Make a slip knot on needle. Place yarn in left hand as shown. Bring needle under front strand of thumb loop (it is between the two loops of thumb), behind and under front strand of forefinger loop, then dip it back between the two strands of thumb loop (under first strand). Let go of the strands on thumb and tighten stitch on needle.

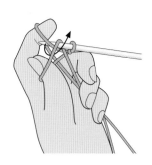

Crochet-Chain Cast On: Use a crochet hook about the same size as the needle being used. Place a slip knot on the crochet hook. Hold the crochet hook in your right hand; the knitting needle in your left hand. Hold the working yarn behind the knitting needle. *Place the hook over the needle and draw a loop with the working yarn through the slip knot on hook. Place working yarn behind needle, and repeat from *. For the last stitch, place the loop from the hook onto the needle.

Provisional Crochet-Chain Cast On: Work as for "Crochet-Chain Cast On" (above), using a smooth waste yarn. When the desired number of stitches are on the needle, chain 3 and fasten off. Put a knot in the tail to remind you that this is the end to pull out. Proceed to knit with main yarn. When live stitches are needed, pick out the first stitch from the knotted tail end, and then carefully unzip the crochet chain, picking up the live stitches on a needle as they pop out.

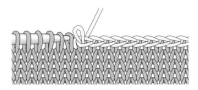

Remove chain one stitch at a time.

Cable-Edge Cast On: Place a slip knot on the left-hand needle. Insert tip of right needle through the loop on left needle and knit a stitch, placing it on the left needle by dipping the left needle under the stitch. *Insert the right needle

between the two stitches and knit a stitch, placing it on the left needle as above*. Repeat from * to *.

Insert needle between two stitches. Knit a stitch.

Place new stitch on left needle.

BINDING OFF

WHILE there are also many methods of binding off, once again, we most likely use the plain old bind off of knit 2, pass the first stitch over the second, knit 1, pass the stitch over, and so on. Providing you do this loosely and neatly, it works just fine. Three-needle bind off is a great method that makes beautifully neat and smooth seams, but can only be used when there are live stitches.

Three-Needle Bind Off: Holding work right side to right side produces an invisible seam; holding work wrong side to wrong side produces a ridge on the right side of the work. Place each set of stitches on a needle with both the points facing the same direction and hold together, one in front, one in back. Insert the right-hand needle (the third needle) through the first stitch on both needles and knit. Repeat for the second stitch, then pass the first stitch over the second as you would do in a normal bind off. Continue binding off in this manner until all stitches are worked.

Knit together one stitch from front needle and one stitch from back needle.

Bind off.

CABLES

Front Cable (C4F): Slip two stitches to cable needle and hold in front of work, work two stitches from needle, then work the two stitches from cable needle.

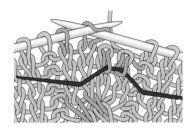

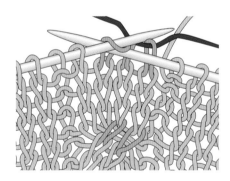

Back Cable (C4B): Work as for front cable but hold cable needle in back of work.

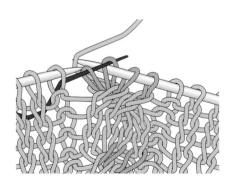

TWISTS

Left Twist (LT): Skip 1 stitch, knit into the back of the second stitch and leave it on the needle; knit both stitches together through the back and slip both from needle.

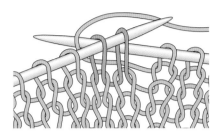

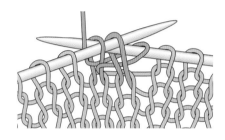

Right Twist (RT): Knit two together and leave them on the needle, then knit first stitch; slip both stitches from needle.

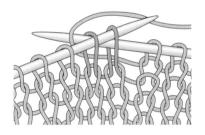

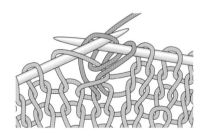

INCREASES

THERE are so many ways to increase, but I find the M1 left or right is a wonderful method. I also specify a backward loop for the Clouds of Purple Shawl and Blue Sky Mittens.

M1: Increase one stitch by slanting either to the right or to the left. If left or right is not specified, you may use either method.

M1 Left (M1L): With left needle, pick up horizontal thread between two stitches from front to back. Knit into back of this loop.

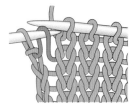 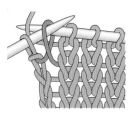

Insert left needle from front to back through "running thread."   Knit into back of stitch.

M1 Right (M1R): With left needle, pick up horizontal thread between two stitches from back to front. Knit into the front of this loop.

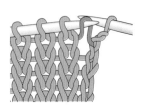 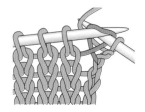

Insert left needle from back to front through "running thread."   Knit into front of stitch.

Backward Loop: Using right forefinger, wrap yarn from back to front; twist finger slightly and slide right needle between finger and yarn. Tighten stitch on needle.

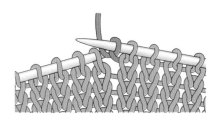

GRAFTING IN STOCKINETTE STITCH

ARRANGE stitches to be grafted on two needles with points facing in the same direction. Hold the work wrong side to wrong side, needles together in left hand. Thread a tapestry needle with at least 1" of yarn for each stitch. Attach yarn to back needle and work right to left. Bring yarn through first stitch on front needle as if to purl and leave the stitch on the needle. Bring the yarn through the first stitch on back needle as if to knit and leave the stitch on the needle. *Bring the yarn through the first stitch on the front needle as if to knit and slip it off the needle; bring the yarn through the next stitch on the front needle as if to purl and leave the stitch on the needle. Bring the yarn through the first stitch on the back needle as if to purl and slip the stitch off the needle. Bring the yarn through the next stitch on the back needle as if to knit and leave the stitch on the needle.* Repeat from * to * until one stitch is left on each needle. Bring yarn through stitch on front needle as if to knit and slip it off. Bring yarn through stitch on back needle as if to purl and slip it off.

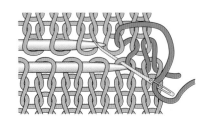

Hems

To MAKE A clean, smooth hem, use a yarn needle to sew the live stitches down. Cut a strand of yarn approximately three times the diameter of the neck opening, and slipstitch each stitch down loosely, covering the selvage remaining from picking up the stitches; fasten off. Be careful not to sew too tightly.

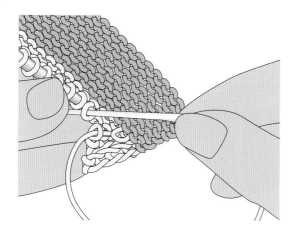

Short-Row Shoulder Shaping

SHOULDER shaping for most patterns one comes across is written in the traditional way. The number of stitches for the shoulder is usually divided by three, and the resulting number is bound off at the beginning of three alternate rows. This produces a "stairstep" that some knitters find unsatisfactory. To eliminate this, you can do short-row shaping. Designs that do not have complicated stitch patterns can easily be worked using this method. The technique of wrapping and turning and hiding wraps is explained below.

Wrap and Turn (W and T)

Right side row: Work the specified number of stitches to where it says "W and T." With yarn in back, slip next stitch purlwise, bring yarn to opposite side of work, slip same stitch back to left needle, turn, bringing yarn to purl side of work. The wrapped stitch will be on right needle. Slip first stitch on left needle and work back.

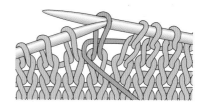

Slip stitch as if to purl. Move yarn
to front of work and slip stitch
back to left needle.

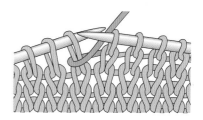

Move yarn to back of work. Turn.

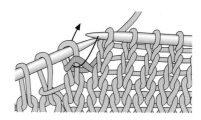

On the final row, knit bar (wrap)
and stitch together.

Wrong side row: Work the specified number of stitches to where it says "W and T." With yarn in front, slip next stitch purlwise, bring yarn to knit side of work, slip same stitch back to left needle, turn, bringing yarn to purl side of work. The wrapped stitch will be on right needle. Slip first stitch on left needle and work back.

Hiding wraps: On subsequent rows, hide wrapped stitch of previous row by inserting point of right needle under wrap and through wrapped stitch, knitting or purling them together.

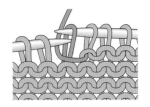

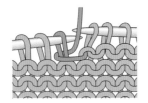

Slip stitch as if to purl. Move yarn to back of work and slip stitch back to left needle.

Move yarn toward you. Turn.

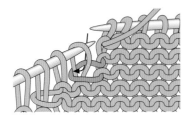

On final row, purl bar (wrap) and stitch together.

Converting a bind-off shoulder to short-row shaping: For an example, we will use the following shoulder-shaping pattern that uses 21 stitches: "Bind off 7 sts at beg of next 3 RS rows."

To convert this example to short-row shaping, we will wrap the last stitch of each group of seven. Therefore , it becomes: "Beg at neck edge, work 13 sts, W and T. Work back. Work 6 sts, W and T, work back. Work across all sts of next row, hiding wraps."

Remember that short-row shaping for shoulders must start at the neck edge, because this is the side that you want to be longer. It will gradually slope down to the armhole edge.

What if the pattern calls for neck-edge shaping at the same time it calls for shoulder shaping? Just incorporate the decreasing into the beginning of the row.

Binding off short-row shaping: If the garment is made from heavy yarn, you may want the extra stability of a sewn shoulder seam. In that case, bind off all stitches across the row after short-row-

ing shaping has been completed, and sew the shoulder seam as usual. If the garment is lightweight, then a three-needle bind off is the perfect finish. After short-row shaping has been completed, put the stitches onto holders and proceed with three-needle bind off.

ONE-ROW BUTTONHOLE

WORK to where the buttonhole begins and proceed as follows:

Slip one stitch purlwise with yarn in front.

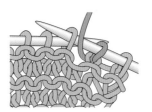

Bring yarn to front. Slip one stitch purlwise.

Place yarn in back and leave it there. *Slip one purlwise, pass previous stitch over it*, rep from * to * for as many stitches as the directions specify.

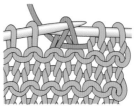

Move yarn to back. Slip another stitch purlwise. Pass first slipped stitch over the second.

Slip last bound-off stitch back to left needle and turn work, putting yarn in back. Cable-edge cast on the same number of stitches as bind off.

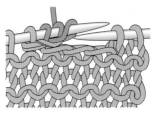

Cast on same number of stitches as bind off.

Cast on one more, but put yarn in front before putting it back on left needle. Turn work. Slip one stitch knitwise and pass extra cast-on stitch over.

TWISTED CORD

CUT A LENGTH of yarn four times the length you wish the cord to be. Double it. Tape one end to a table or have someone hold it. Begin twisting until you see the cord start to kink. Still holding the end taut with one hand, take your other hand and bend the cord in the center, letting the two sides twist around each other. Knot both ends of the cord.

CROCHET

Chain (ch): Place a slip stitch on hook. Holding hook in right hand and tensioning yarn in left as shown, draw working yarn through slip stitch on hook. Repeat for the desired number of chains.

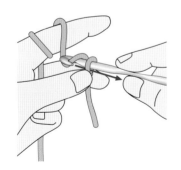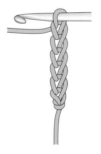

Single crochet (sc): *Insert hook under the two top threads of the stitch. Yarn over hook and draw it through the stitch. There are now two loops on hook. Yarn over hook and draw it through both loops on hook*. Repeat from * to * for the desired number of single crochets.

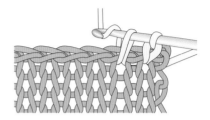

Insert hook into stitch, yarn over hook, pull loop through to front, yarn over hook. Pull loop through both loops on hook.

Double crochet (dc): *Yarn over hook, insert hook under the two top threads of stitch, yarn over hook and draw it through the stitch. There are now three loops on hook. Yarn over hook and draw it through two loops on hook. Yarn over hook and draw it through remaining two loops on hook*. Repeat from * to * for the desired number of double crochets.

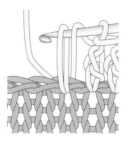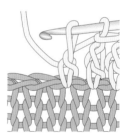

Yarn over hook, insert hook into stitch, yarn over hook, pull through to front.

Yarn over hook, pull through two loops on hook.

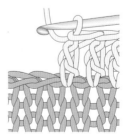

Yarn over hook, pull through remaining two loops on hook.

Fiber Care

A GOOD GENERAL RULE is to care for any garment as if it were wool. Hand wash it in tepid water; do not subject it to drastic changes in water temperature; do not agitate, wring, or twist; and always support the weight of the wet garment. The only exception to the above rule is 100% linen or hemp, which can be machine washed and dried. If the fiber is a blend, then it must be treated by the general rule.

MOHAIR, ALPACA, AND LLAMA

DRY FLAT, and do not press with an iron. You may hover the iron over the item and mist with steam, but pressing will flatten the lovely haze of the fiber. Try to avoid ripping out stitches in any mohair yarn. It gives the shorter fibers a chance to slip out of the twist, making the yarn fluffier.

SILK

DO NOT use an iron on high heat. Doing so will weaken the fabric. When I need to press silk, I hover my steam iron over the fabric but never press the iron directly onto it. If you're steaming a lace pattern, you may stretch the lace as much or as little as you wish.

ANGORA

DO NOT pack angora articles tightly in a drawer—the beautiful haze will become matted down. Wash very carefully by hand in tepid water, being careful to never agitate. In general, just think of soaking them. Do not even think of the word *swish*. Lay them flat to dry, and do not press directly with an iron, as it will flatten the lovely haze.

QIVIUT

DO NOT press qiviut directly with an iron. Doing so will flatten the lovely fluff.

COTTON

HAND wash cotton garments in cool water—do not wring or twist—and lay flat to dry away from sunlight and heat.

LINEN AND HEMP

CARE for 100% hemp and linen garments by machine washing and machine drying, taking the garment from the dryer just before it is totally dry. Lay flat to finish drying.

BLENDS

CARE for blends as you would any fine garment. Hand wash in gentle soap, rinse thoroughly, do not wring, and lay flat to dry away from direct sun and heat.

Resources

Edelweiss Jacket
Buckwheat Bridge Angora
18 Buckwheat Bridge Road
Germantown, NY 12526
Phone: 518-537-4487
Fax: 518-537-6099
Email: slhdem@webjogger.net

Bouclé Swing Coat
Oak Grove Yarns
PO Box 531, Pine Banks Road
Putney, VT 05346
Email: oakgrove@sover.net

Clouds of Purple Shawl, Cornflower Cardigan, Beaded Pulse Warmers
Knit One, Crochet Too (K1C2) Yarns and Patterns
7 Commons Avenue, Ste 2
Windham, ME 04062
www.knitonecrochettoo.com

Blue Sky Mittens and Hat, Ice Blue Shell
PO Box 387
St. Francis, MN 55070
Toll free: 888-460-8862
Web site: www.blueskyalpacas.com

Llama Cables
Cascade Yarns
PO Box 58168
Tukwila, WA 98138
Toll free: 800-548-1048 (call for dealer nearest you)
Phone: 206-574-0440
Fax: 888-855-9276

Hooded Scarf and Mittens
Mountain Colors
PO Box 156
Corvallis, MT 59828
Phone: 406-777-3377 (call for dealer nearest you)
Fax: 406-777-7313
Email: info@mountaincolors.com
Web site: www.mountaincolors.com

Razor Shell Shawl
Rabbit Tree Farm
130 Jack Road
Saxonburg, PA 16056
Phone: 742-352-4832
Email: ogoat@nauticom.net

Caroline's Sweater
Sweaterkits.com
P.O Box 397
Sharon, Ontario
Canada L0G 1V0
Toll free: 1-877-232-9415
Email: mail@sweaterkits.com
Web site: www.sweaterkits.com

Star Stitch Twin Set
Lorna's Laces Yarns
4229 North Honore Street
Chicago, IL 60613
773-935-3803
Web site: www.lornaslaces.net
(wholesale only, contact dealer near you)

Magic Colors Silk Stole
Charlene Schurch
12165 Helm Lane SW
Moore Haven, FL 33471
Phone: 863-674-0790
Email: caloosa@juno.com

Smocked Vest
Skacel Collection, Inc.
PO Box 88110
Seattle, WA 98138-2110
Phone: 253-854-2710 (call for dealer nearest you)
Fax: 253-854-2571
Web site: www.skacelknitting.com

Muffatees
Ken Abert
Kevin Street
Dorchester Farms
8 Florida Street
Dorchester, MA 02124
Phone: 617-436-5758
Fax: 617-822-0003
Email: Dorfarms@aol.com

Lucinda Shells Shawl
Susan Emerson
Enchanted Lace Yarns
Phone: 303-641-8463
Email: lacelady@mindspring.com

Curry Cockleshell Scarf
Yarn Barn of Kansas
930 Massachusetts
Lawrence, KS 66044
Toll free: 800-468-0035

John and Dianne Nash
HC04 Box 9220
Palmer, AK 99645
Phone: 907-745-1005
Email: nashfarm@alaska.com
Web site: www.windyvalleymuskox.com

Autumn in New England Pullover
Crystal Palace Yarns/Straw into Gold
2320 Bissell Avenue
Richmond, CA 94804
Phone: 510-237-9988
Web site: www.straw.com

Sage Short-Sleeved Pullover, Haneke Red Pullover, White Winter Pullover, Heavenly Blue Cardigan
Haneke Wool Fashions
630 North Blackcat Road
Meridian, ID 83642
Toll free: 1-800-523-WOOL

Sunflower Shell
Westminster Fibers, Inc.
4 Townsend West, Unit 8
Nashua, NH 03063
Phone: 603-886-5041 (call for dealer nearest you)
Fax: 603-886-1056
Email: wfibers@aol.com

Willow Linen Pullover, Lucinda Shells Shawl
Louet Sales
808 Commerce Park Drive
Ogdensburg, NY, 13669
Phone: 613-925-4502 (call for dealer nearest
you)
Email: info@louet.com

Master of Linen
European Linen of Quality
15.Rue Du Louvre
Boite 71
F-75001 Paris, France
Phone: 33 (0) 1 42 21 06 83
Fax: 33 (0) 1 42 21 48 22
Email: info@mastersoflinen.com
Web site: www.Mastersoflinen.com

Striped Market Bag
Lana Hames
Lanaknits Designs' Hemp for Knitting
105 Park Street
Nelson BC V1L 2G5
Toll free: 1-888-301-0011
Email: info@lanaknits.com
Web site: www.lanaknits.com

Buttons
Custom Made Buttons
Jenny Olson
4385 Driving Range Road
Corona, CA 92883
Phone: 909-372-0642

The Wool Connection
34 E. Main Street
Avon, CT 06001
Phone: 860-678-1710
Fax: 860-677-7039
Email: wool@tiac.net
Web site: www.woolconnection.com

Bibliography

Amedro, Gladys. *Shetland Lace*. Lerwick, Shetland, U.K: The Shetland Times Ltd., 1996.

L. P. Brockett. *The Silk Industry in America: A History*. The Silk Association of America, 1876.

Compton, Rae. *The Illustrated Dictionary of Knitting*. Loveland, Colo.: Interweave Press, 1988.

Crockett, Candace. *The Complete Spinning Book*. New York: Watson-Guptill Publications, 1977.

Hoffman, Eric, and Murray E. Fowler. *The Alpaca Book*. Jackson, Calif.: Clay Press Inc., 1995.

Jones, Lem. *Raising Angora Goats—Then and Now, 1849–1995*. Tex.: Nortex Press.

Kilfoyle, Sharon, and Leslie B. Samson. *Completely Angora*. Samson Angoras, 1992.

Kolander, Cheryl. *A Silk Worker's Notebook*. Loveland, Colo.: Interweave Press, 1985.

Potter, Beatrix. *The Tale of Benjamin Bunny*. New York: Frederick Warne and Co., 1904.

Romcke, Kirsten, and Nina Granlund Sæther. Translation by Arnhild H. Hillesland. *Pearls on the Pulse*. Norges Husflidslag, 2001.

Stanfield, Lesley. *The New Knitting Stitch Library*. Asheville, N.C.: Lark Books, 1998.

Stanley, Montse. *Reader's Digest Knitter's Handbook*. Pleasantville, N. Y.: Reader's Digest, 1993.

Swansen, Meg. *Meg Swansen's Knitting*. Loveland, Colo.: Interweave Press, 1999.

Textiles in New England 1790–1840. Sturbridge, Mass.: Old Sturbridge Village Booklet Series, 1961.

Acknowledgments

While countless people have helped me through all the phases of writing this book, my knitting students have been the most encouraging. Their gratitude for my work makes it all worth the effort. Special thanks to Suzanne Federer, who helped knit some of the items.

Thanks to Sarah Coe for standing by my side during rough times. Many thanks to my editor, Ursula Reikes, for everything about this book, and to Karen Soltys and all the other wonderful people at Martingale who worked on it.

My dear knitting friends have been beside me constantly, cheering me on every time I whined, and basically saying to me, "Just hurry up and get it done already." I am fortunate to have three Judys in my life: my sister, Judith Eisner; my fellow knitwear designer and teacher, Judy Pascale; and my wonderful friend, Judy Anderson. Although her name is not Judy, Charlene Schurch is included here, as she has always given me her best advice, asked for or not. I treasure you all more than I can say, and thanks for making this book happen. I could not have done it without you.

Thanks to my friends who have known me the longest: Dody and Mitch Knight, Lenore Grunko, Patrick McGlamery, Dahlia Popovitz, Steven and Edith Daigle, and Donna McLaughlin.

For all my cello students—past, present, and future—I thank you for keeping me on my toes and making me proud.

I am indebted to the people who have generously contributed their time, expertise, yarn, and/or accessories: Marilyn Ackley, Wendy Pieh, Yvonne Taylor, Ann Galonska, Myrna Stahman, John and Dianne Nash, Sara Healy and Dan Melamed, Linda MacMillan, Linda Niemeyer, Kathy Haneke, Gloria Tracy, Diana McKay, Leslie Taylor, Marilyn and Paul Merbach, Caroline McInnis, Lorna Miser, Charlene Schurch, Susan Emerson, Ingrid Skacel, Ken Abert, Kenneth and June Bridgewater, Susan and Jim Bateman, Trudy and Jan van Stralen, Lana Hames, Cascacde Yarns, Crystal Palace Yarns, Masters of Linen, Phyllis and Bob Fishberg, and Jenny Olsen. Information about these people and their yarns can be found in "Resources" on page 135.

Thank you to professors Charles Henry, David Wagner, and Greg Anderson, of the University of Connecticut, for supplying me with photos.

Thanks to my family: my parents, Raymond and Sarah Eisner, who taught me the love of using my hands to create beautiful things, and my three sons—Nathaniel, Liam, and Noah—who taught me patience.

And Ken, my husband and best friend. The list of things you do for me is endless. Your patience keeps me sane. You always know just what to say and when to say it, and have learned that when asked for color advice, it's always safe to say "blue." Thank you for 28 years—and more to come—of happiness.

Knitting and Crochet Titles

ACCESSORIES

Crocheted Pursenalities

Crocheted Socks!

Kitty Knits

Pursenalities

Pursenality Plus

Stitch Style: Mittens

BABIES, CHILDREN & TOYS

Berets, Beanies, and Booties

Crochet for Tots

Gigi Knits…and Purls—*NEW!*

Knitting with Gigi

Too Cute!

CROCHET

365 Crochet Stitches a Year:
    Perpetual Calendar

Amigurumi World

A to Z of Crochet

First Crochet

KNITTING

200 Knitted Blocks

365 Knitting Stitches a Year:
    Perpetual Calendar

A to Z of Knitting

Cable Confidence—*NEW!*

Casual, Elegant Knits—*NEW!*

Chic Knits

Fair Isle Sweaters Simplified

First Knits

Handknit Skirts

Handknit Style II

Knit One, Stripe Too

The Knitter's Book of
    Finishing Techniques

Knitting Beyond the Basics

Modern Classics

Ocean Breezes

Romantic Style

Silk Knits

Simple Gifts for Dog Lovers

Skein for Skein—*NEW!*

Special Little Knits from
    Just One Skein

Stripes, Stripes, Stripes

Top Down Sweaters

Wrapped in Comfort

The Yarn Stash Workbook

LITTLE BOX SERIES

The Little Box of Crochet for
    Baby

The Little Box of Crocheted Gifts

The Little Box of
    Crocheted Scarves

The Little Box of
    Crocheted Throws

The Little Box of Knits for Baby

The Little Box of Knitted Gifts

The Little Box of Knitted Throws

The Little Box of Socks

SOCK KNITTING

Knitting Circles around Socks

More Sensational Knitted Socks

Sensational Knitted Socks

Stitch Style: Socks

Martingale® & COMPANY

America's Best-Loved Craft & Hobby Books®
America's Best-Loved Knitting Books®

Our books are available at bookstores and your favorite craft, fabric, and yarn retailers. If you don't see the title you're looking for, visit us at **www.martingale-pub.com** or contact us at:

1-800-426-3126

International: 1-425-483-3313
Fax: 1-425-486-7596 • **Email:** info@martingale-pub.com